101
things
to do
OUTSIDE

Quarto is the authority on a wide range of topics.
Quarto educates, entertains, and enriches the lives of our readers—
enthusiasts and lovers of hands-on living.
www.quartoknows.com

Published by Walter Foster Jr. Publishing,
an imprint of Quarto Publishing Group USA Inc.
All rights reserved. Walter Foster Jr. is a registered
trademark.

First published in Great Britain in 2015 by Weldon Owen.

6 Orchard Road, Suite 100
Lake Forest, CA 92630
quartoknows.com
Visit our blogs @quartoknows.com

Printed in Malaysia
1 3 5 7 9 10 8 6 4 2

101
things
to do
OUTSIDE

CONTENTS

1 ATTRACT BUTTERFLIES

Tempt butterflies into your garden or onto your balcony with a butterfly feeder. It's simple to make and works like a dream.

YOU WILL NEED:

- Paper plate
- Scissors
- String
- Overripe (mushy) fruit

1 Make four holes around the rim of your paper plate. They should be equally spaced, just like the hour, half-past, quarter-past and quarter-of positions on a clock face.

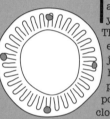

2 Cut four equal lengths of string and double knot the ends. Thread the string through the holes in your plate, making sure that the knots are underneath the plate. Tie the ends of the string together at the top.

3 Chop some overripe fruit and put it onto the plate. Butterflies particularly like squishy banana! (If you put a banana in your refrigerator, it will go black and mushy more quickly.) Now hang up your feeder, and wait for some butterfly visitors!

TOP TIP

Plant flowers to attract butterflies too! Sunflowers are great because butterflies love them!

DONE! DATE COMPLETED

CALCULATE HOW CLOSE A STORM IS

If you like storms, you'll love this! But remember to stay safe. If the storm is overhead, enjoy it from a safe place indoors.

1 On a stormy day, watch out for a flash of lightning in the sky.

2 As soon as you see the lightning, count the number of seconds until you hear the thunder. To be really precise, use a stopwatch. Or be as accurate as you can by counting like this: one-one thousand, two-one thousand, three-one thousand, etc.

3 For every 5 seconds, the storm is 1 mile away (or for every 3 seconds, it is 1 km away). Divide the number of seconds you count to work out the distance.

HOW DOES IT WORK?
Thunder and lightning happen at the same time, but light travels more quickly than sound. The light of the lightning flash travels more quickly than the sound of the thunder.

DONE!   DATE COMPLETED

3 GROW PIZZA SAUCE

OK, so you'll need to supply the pizza base and the cheese separately, but you can grow all of the ingredients for a truly delicious pizza sauce in just five to six weeks!

YOU WILL NEED:

- Big container (ideally 1 foot deep) with drainage holes
- Compost
- Trowel
- 3 stakes or bamboo canes
- Garden string
- Pebbles or sticks
- Plants:
  Tomato, onion, dwarf pepper, basil, chives, thyme, oregano
- Watering can

1 Put your container in a sunny spot and fill with compost, leaving 1 inch free at the top. Make sure that your plants are well watered in the containers that they came in.

2 First, plant the tomato. Dig a hole in the center of the container that is slightly deeper than the tomato plant's pot. Plant the tomato carefully, pressing the soil down around its roots.

3 Divide the pot into six "slices" with your sticks or pebbles. Dig a hole for each plant in a different "slice." Unlike the tomato, the holes should be the same depth as their old pots.

4 If the plant has been in a small pot for a long time, the roots might be packed tightly together. You can carefully pull them apart with your fingertips. But be very gentle!

5 Plant the vegetables and herbs. Make sure that you press the soil down around the roots. The bottom of the stems should be at the same level as the top of the soil. Put labels next to each plant so that you remember which is which.

6 Push the stakes into your container. Space them apart equally, near to the edge. Tie them together at the top like a teepee with garden string. Take care not to disturb your plants. Carefully tie the tomato plant to the sticks, making sure not to tie them too tightly. You just want to tie them so that they can grow upward and not fall over from the weight of the tomatoes.

7 Keep your pizza garden well watered, and watch it grow. Harvest your crop when it's ready to make an extremely delicious pizza sauce!

DONE! DATE COMPLETED

4 FRAME YOUR DAY

When you next go the beach, take along a camera and snap a few selfies. If your beach allows it, collect shells, pebbles, and other interesting things to take home with you.

YOU WILL NEED:

- Shells and pebbles collected from the beach
- Flat picture frame
- Pencil
- Craft glue

1 When you get home, lay your treasures on the ground outside to see what you've found. You might need to brush off the sand and wash them down before you use them. Pick out the best bits.

2 Arrange your treasures onto the picture frame. Play around with the design until it's exactly how you want it, then glue everything onto the frame with craft glue.

3 Print your best selfie and put it in the frame. What better way to remember a fun day at the beach? It could make a great present, too!

DONE!   DATE COMPLETED

TALK BY FLASHLIGHT

Before satellites, Morse code was used by almost everyone needing to send messages over long distances. It helped to save lives and to win wars. Get together with a friend and give it a try with a flashlight. It might take longer than texting, but it's a lot of fun!

1 Before dark, you should both practice without the flashlight. Write messages in dots and dashes on paper, and pass them to each other to decipher. Use the chart below to work out each letter. Keep the messages short and snappy. For example:

HELLO

INTERNATIONAL MORSE CODE ALPHABET

A •−	J •−−−	S •••	1 •−−−−
B −•••	K −•−	T −	2 ••−−−
C −•−•	L •−••	U ••−	3 •••−−
D −••	M −−	V •••−	4 ••••−
E •	N −•	W •−−	5 •••••
F ••−•	O −−−	X −••−	6 −••••
G −−•	P •−−•	Y −•−−	7 −−•••
H ••••	Q −−•−	Z −−••	8 −−−••
I ••	R •−•		9 −−−−•
			0 −−−−−

2 After dark, send messages with your flashlights. Stand at either end of a garden or path, and use long flashes for the dashes and short flashes for the dots. If you're receiving the message, write down the dots and dashes on paper so that you can decipher them with the international Morse code alphabet.

DONE!   DATE COMPLETED

6 BOB FOR APPLES

Traditionally a Halloween game, this is great fun on any occasion—you just need a bowl of water and some apples. Be warned, though, you WILL get wet!

1 Put a bowl onto something sturdy at roughly waist height, like a strong outdoor table. Fill it three-fourths full with water and float the apples on the top. Add as many apples as will fit, but not so many that they can't move around in the water.

2 Players must put their hands behind their backs while trying to catch an apple between their teeth. Decide how long each player has—for example, 20 seconds. All other players should count them down by saying one-Mississippi, two-Mississippi, and so on.

3 When a player has caught an apple, the counting stops and that is their score. Everyone takes a turn, and the person with the lowest score wins!

DONE! DATE COMPLETED

PLAY SAY AND CATCH

For this game you need a soft ball, some friends, and quick reactions, so make sure to stay alert!

1 Before starting the game, decide on a category—e.g., animals, pop music, beach, school, etc. To begin the game, all stand in a circle at least 3 feet away from one another.

2 Take it in turns to throw the ball to another player. Before catching the ball, each player must say a word that has something to do with the chosen category. So, if the category is animals, they might say "cat." Words can only be used once!

3 Anyone who drops the ball, doesn't come up with a word from the category, or repeats a word that's already been used is out of the game.

4 The last player standing is the winner. Now, choose a different category for a new round!

DONE! DATE COMPLETED

8 MAKE A SEASHELL PET

Next time you're on the beach, collect shells to take home. Try to find different shapes and sizes, and make sure there aren't any creatures left inside!

YOU WILL NEED:

- A collection of shells
- Craft glue
- Paintbrush
- Modeling clay
- Small beads

1 Take a look at these shell creatures. Are any of them cute enough to be your pet? Use them as inspiration as you sift through your shell collection to find shapes and sizes that you could use.

2 Experiment with different shell combinations before gluing them together. Modeling clay is a great way to fix them in position while you get your glue ready. Build the heads and bodies separately, and glue on smaller parts, like eyes, ears, and noses before joining them to the other bits. If you don't have any tiny shells for eyes and noses, you can use beads.

3 When you're happy with your arrangement, glue it together. Use the brush to paint glue onto the more delicate pieces. The clay is also useful to support your pet while it dries.

DONE! DATE COMPLETED

PHOTOGRAPH THE ALPHABET

When you're out and about, either in the city or the countryside, find and collect your very own alphabet. If you look carefully, letters are everywhere, even in the most unexpected places.

1 Go for a walk in your neighborhood to begin the letter hunt. Always take an adult with you, or let one know where you're going. First of all look for the obvious letters on signs, stores, and cars. When you see a letter that you like the look of, take a photo of it. Try to capture just the letter without anything else around it.

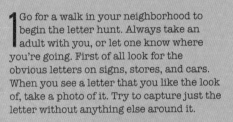

2 Now look for less obvious letters. There are lots of shapes in buildings, plants, and all sorts of objects that look like different letters. The letter "E" might be half a window frame or a gate, a set of traffic lights, or the shadow of some telephone lines.

3 Then, make your own letters. You might trace them in the sand or the earth, or you might lay them out with leaves and pinecones or paperclips and pens. You could even ask a friend to make the shape of a letter with his or her body.

4 Try to collect the whole alphabet. Then, print them out to write messages to your friends. They're great for interesting greeting cards, and especially impressive on valentines!

DONE!   DATE COMPLETED

10 TRY CHINESE JUMP ROPE

For this ancient Chinese game, you'll need skipping elastic and two friends. Stay focused and you might complete all three levels!

1 Decide which two of you are the "enders." If you're the jumper, then stand with the elastic around your ankles and feet shoulder-width apart. Be far enough away from each other for the elastic to be pulled tight above the ground.

2 The third person is the jumper. Start with your feet inside the rope, in the middle of the "enders."

3 Jump with both feet out. Then jump with both feet back in.

4 Jump so the right foot lands on the rope, and the left foot lands outside it. Do this again, but the other way around with the left foot on the rope, and the right foot outside it.

5 Jump so that both feet land on the rope. If you've completed this without missing a step or standing on the elastic when you shouldn't have, you've completed level 1!

6 For level 2, the enders lift the elastic to calf height, and the jumper tries to complete the sequence again. If at any point the jumper misses a step or stands on the elastic, it's someone else's turn, and the jumper and ender swap places.

7 Don't worry if you have to swap—it'll be your turn again soon, and you can start from where you left off. See if you can get to level 3, which is knee height. The winner is the first to complete all levels.

WHY NOT?
When you've played levels 1–3, you can try levels 4 and 5, where the rope is at mid-thigh and thigh-high level. Can you jump that high?

DONE!

DATE COMPLETED

11 PLAY GLOW-IN-THE-DARK RING TOSS

Have you ever played glow-in-the-dark ring toss? All you need are a few empty drink bottles, a bunch of glow sticks (12 inches and 6 inches long), and a couple of friends. How good is your aim?

1 Wait until dark. Fill each bottle three-fourths full with water. Bend and shake the 6 smaller glow sticks to activate them. Drop 1 into each bottle. Screw on the bottle tops.

2 Each player should now take 5 to 10 of the longer glow sticks and their connectors and make them into rings. Bend and shake them to activate the glow.

3 Set the bottles about 1 foot apart, in a triangular shape. Decide on your throwing line and all stand behind it.

4 Now play! Take it in turns to use all your rings to get as many points as possible. You get 3 points for each ring that lands over a bottle, and 1 point for a ring that touches a bottle. Remember to keep behind the throwing line!

DONE!   DATE COMPLETED

SPRAY A RAINBOW

You might not find a pot of gold, but you can make your own rainbow on a sunny day with a garden hose.

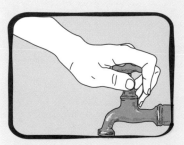

1 Check with an adult that it's OK to use the hose before you start. Find a sunny spot to hold the hose, and turn the tap on.

2 Turn until your back is facing the sun. You can check your position by making sure that your shadow is in front of you.

3 Put your thumb over the nozzle to create a misty spray. Hold the hose out in front of you and turn slowly. Keep your thumb over the nozzle, and watch for a rainbow to appear in the spray!

DONE!

DATE COMPLETED

13 BUILD A WILLOW TUNNEL

For a shady retreat, build a willow tunnel. Once you've got the hang of it, you could also try a dome. Or build a willow complex, joining domes and tunnels together!

YOU WILL NEED:

For a 12-foot tunnel

- 26 stems of heavy willow for the uprights, and another 12 for the horizontal walls.
  (available from a garden center)
- Spade
- Tape measure
- Garden string

1 Decide where you will do this. Always make sure that you have permission to use the land. Now prepare the site. Use a spade to dig two trenches, 3 to 4 feet apart, 12 inches wide and deep.

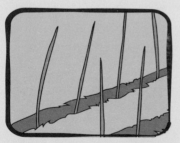

2 Plant the uprights. You will need 13 willow stems for each trench. Plant them about 1 foot apart. Push each about 1 foot into the ground. You might want an adult to help you to do this if the ground isn't very soft.

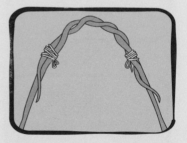

3 Bend each opposite pair of willow stems to form an arch. Twist them together. Fasten with string. You now have the main arch.

4 Now add the horizontals. Start at one end, about half a foot up, and carefully weave a single stem through the uprights. Use a behind, in front, behind, in front type pattern. Use the rest of your rods to weave horizontally on both sides of the tunnel, spacing them equally. Secure them all with string.

5 Give the tunnel a good watering. Keep it well watered. In spring, the first shoots should appear.

DON'T FORGET

You need to make your tunnel when the willow rods are dormant—after leaf fall, and before leaf bud. After you've bought the willow stems, make a start as soon as you can.

6 You can either let your tunnel grow shaggy and wild or ask an adult to help you to neaten it up with garden shears. You should ask an adult to help you cut it back each fall or winter with garden shears in either case. Never use shears on your own.

DONE!   DATE COMPLETED

14 GET THE GOAL!

Ever dreamed of scoring goals like Cristiano Ronaldo? It'll take a bit of practice! Get your soccer career going in your yard or local park.

1 Chalk goalposts onto the wall at different heights and widths. Mark the scores onto the wall—write 10 points for the easiest, 50 points for the hardest, and so on.

2 Mark a kick line for you to place the ball. Aim at the goalposts to win the points. Chalk your points on the pavement.

REMEMBER
Don't forget to wash off the chalk marks afterward—especially if you are using a public space.

3 After 10 kicks, add up your scores. How did you do? Take another 10 kicks, and see if you can beat your original score.

DONE!   DATE COMPLETED

THROW A MONSTER MURAL

You can just "throw" this one together. It's super-easy to create a super-size mural with just paint and play balls.

YOU WILL NEED:

- Large roll of paper or canvas
- Dust sheet or old sheet
- Thumb tacks or clothespins
- Tempera paint
- Paint trays or disposable containers
- Textured play balls, for example, spike balls
- Permanent markers
- Googly eyes (optional)

1 Find a place to hang your paper or canvas. A shed wall or fence is ideal. Check with the owner that it's OK first, though. Canvases can also hang from a washing line. Spread out the dustsheet in front.

2 Squeeze different colored paints into different containers. Roll a ball into one of the paints until it is covered. Stand about 5 feet from the paper and throw the ball.

3 Throw more and more balls until the paper is suitably splattered. You can "sign" it by dipping your hand into the paint and pressing it onto the corner of the paper.

4 Now get creative with the marker pens and googly eyes to make silly, serious, and seriously silly monster faces.

DONE!

DATE COMPLETED

16 DIG A DINOSAUR PARK

Ferns have been around since the dinosaurs roamed the earth, so it makes sense to use them to make your very own Jurassic Park. Let your imagination and the dinosaurs roam . . .

YOU WILL NEED:

- Toy dinosaurs
- Old car tire (ask for an old one at a auto-repair shop)
- Outdoor paint
- Black garbage bags
- Bag of compost
- Prehistoric-looking plants, for example, ferns
- Moss or garden gravel
- Rocks and pebbles

1 Wash the tire. Make sure it's dry before painting the outside. To get a good, strong color, you may need several coats. Let the paint dry between coats. Dry completely overnight.

2 Put the tire in a shady spot where the ferns will grow well. Line the tire with garbage bags, making a few drainage holes in the bottom. Fill with compost.

3 Plant the ferns and water them. Add rocks and pebbles. You might want to pile up soil to make volcanoes, or add blue gravel as a lake. Cover the rest of the soil with moss or gravel.

DONE! DATE COMPLETED

4 Now all you need to do is add the dinosaurs!

PLAY A BOTTLE XYLOPHONE

Become a music maestro with just a collection of old bottles, some water, and a good set of lungs. Glass bottles work best, but plastic will work too.

1 Place your bottles in a line about 2-4 inches apart. Pour a little water into the first bottle, a little more in the second, and so on, until all the bottles have a different amount of water.

2 Blow across the tops of each bottle one after the other to listen to the different pitches. To make a musical scale, place the bottles in order from the one that makes the lowest sound to the one that makes the highest sound. (You may need to remove water from or add water to some of the bottles.)

3 When you're happy with your scale, try to blow a simple tune that you know. See if you can "play" something you know well, such as, "Row, Row, Row Your Boat." Try another. Now make up your own song!

DONE!   DATE COMPLETED

18 SHOOT A BOW AND ARROW

Make mini bows and arrows, and perfect your aim. It'll take practice, but don't give up—even Katniss Everdeen had to start somewhere!

YOU WILL NEED:

- Craft sticks
- Cotton swabs
- Dental floss
- Nail scissors
- Adult help

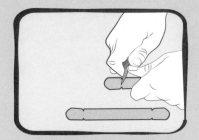

1 Ask an adult to carve notches into your craft sticks with the scissors. Working about half an inch from the ends, you need a notch on each side, on both ends. You should have four notches on each stick.

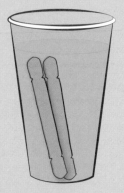

2 Put your sticks into a cup of warm water. Leave for at least an hour. This will soften the wood, allowing it to bend.

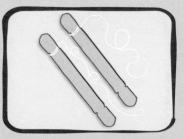

3 Remove the sticks from the water and dry them off. Wrap dental floss around one end of each stick about four times. Knot in place, leaving the rest of the floss to wrap around the other end of the stick.

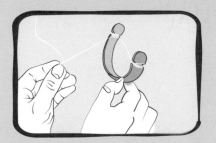

4 Holding the stick in one hand, stretch the dental floss to the notch on the other end. Make sure that you keep the floss on the same side. Carefully bend the stick as you stretch the floss tightly across it.

5 Wrap the floss around the notch at the other end of the stick about four times, and knot it in place. Your bow is ready!

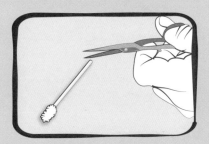

6 To make the arrows, simply snip one end off your cotton swabs with nail scissors. Ask an adult to help you to do this.

7 Aim and FIRE! Line up rows of targets to practice on. They'll need to be small and light, such as toy figurines or pinecones. As you get better at hitting your targets, position them farther and farther away.

DONE! DATE COMPLETED

19 GROW POTATOES IN A BAG

Mashed potato, baked potato, french fries? Yum! Get yourself some potatoes and get growing! If you can, you should "chit" your potatoes first—put them with the "eyes" facing upward in an egg carton for four to six weeks, and wait for them to sprout.

1 Take an old compost bag, and fill one-quarter of it with potting compost. Roll down the sides and carefully poke drainage holes into the bag with a knife. Keep the holes small so that you don't split the bag.

2 Put your potatoes on top with their "eyes" (the sprouted parts) up. Cover them with a little more compost, just to keep them in the dark. Water well and keep in a warm, sunny spot away from frost.

3 As green growth comes up, bury the foliage with more soil and roll a bit more of the bag up to accommodate. You'll need to do this every three to four weeks.

4 After 90 to 100 days, the potato plant will flower, and your crop will be ready to harvest. All you need to do now is tip the bag on its side (outside!) and shake out your potatoes. The only difficulty will be deciding how to cook them!

DONE! DATE COMPLETED

MAKE POTATO PRINTS

20

Potatoes are great to print with, but you can use other homegrown or bought veggies too. Try halving bell peppers and cauliflowers, and experiment with celery leaves and carrot tops.

1 Cut a large potato in half and press a cookie cutter into the center of the potato.

2 Ask an adult to slice around the cookie cutter. Remove the excess potato and the cookie cutter.

3 Squeeze the paint into the saucer and dip the potato into the paint. Press your potato shape onto the paper you want to decorate. Try doing this with your other vegetables too, and see what amazing artwork you can come up with!

DONE!

DATE COMPLETED

21 PUT ON A CLOTHESLINE ART SHOW

You don't need a huge space to set up an outdoor art studio—a balcony, patio, porch, or small lawn will do.

YOU WILL NEED:

- A clothesline or rope
- Pegs
- Paper
- Art materials
- Blanket and cushions (optional)

1 Set up your studio. It can be as simple as a pile of paper and a pot of colored pencils on a rug. A few cushions might be nice too.

2 Be sure to ask an adult to help you to put up the washing line or tie a rope between two posts or trees. It should be at a height that you can reach. Put a bag or box of pegs near the line.

3 Ask a few friends to come and make some art. Pin your masterpieces to the line as you do them. Now invite more friends or your family to your art show.

DONE!   DATE COMPLETED

RELAX WITH YOGA

22

Find a quiet spot in a garden, in the park, or at the beach, and try some of these basic yoga moves. Repeat them as many times as you feel comfortable.

1 Sit cross-legged. Raise one hand into a fist. Breathe in while counting to 5 and uncurling your fingers. Breathe out to the count of 5 while slowly curling your fingers back into your fist. Repeat on the other side.

2 Stand straight with your legs spread out and your arms at your sides. Breathe out and bring your right arm over your head while the left arm slides down your left leg. Repeat on the other side.

3 Stand straight with your hands closed above your head. Breathe in deeply. Stare ahead. Breathe out, bending one leg slightly as the other comes up to rest the foot just below the knee of the standing leg. Hold as long as possible. Bring the bent leg down. Rest. Repeat.

4 Lie flat on the floor with your arms and legs stretched out. Breathe out and lift your arms and legs a couple of inches above the ground. Stay as long as you feel comfortable, then rest and try again.

DONE! DATE COMPLETED

23 PLAY FROGS AND FLIES

Are any of your friends super sleuths? Maybe one or two are heading for a career on the stage? If so, they'll enjoy this game.

1 Sit in a circle and choose a Detective. This person must now go away from the group, out of earshot, until her or she is called back. Now decide who is going to be the Frog. Everyone else is a fly.

2 Call the Detective back. The Frog is going to "kill" the flies secretly while the Detective isn't looking by sticking his or her tongue out at them.

3 The flies should "die" as dramatically as possible, with lots of spinning and buzzing. They eventually fall into a heap on the floor.

4 The Detective needs to work out who the Frog is before the flies are killed off. If the Frog eats all the flies but one, he or she wins. If the Detective guesses who the Frog is before that, he or she wins. But the Detective only has 3 guesses.

5 For a new game, start all over again with a new Detective.

WHY NOT?
If there's quite a large group of you, you could also select a Fly Saver. This is a person who can bring the flies back to life with a special signal (for example, pointing). But if the Detective works out who the Fly Saver is, then he or she also becomes a dead fly.

DONE! DATE COMPLETED

24 THROW A SEEDBALL

"Throw it, grow it," is the seedballer's mantra. You can literally throw a garden into a place that needs a little bit of life and color!

YOU WILL NEED:

- Seeds (easy-to-grow or native varieties)
- Clay (available from craft stores)
- Compost or potting soil
- Mixing bowl or bucket
- Spoon
- Water

1 Select seeds that are easy-to-grow without too much water or pampering. If you're mixing, choose plants that will look good together when they flower. Soak the seeds overnight and drain away the water in the morning.

2 It's best to mix your ingredients outdoors, as it can be quite messy. You need 5 cups of clay, 1 cup of compost, and 1 cup of seeds. Your cups can be as big or small as you like as long as you stick to these ratios—5:1:1. Put the seeds and compost into your bowl and mix with the spoon.

3 Mix in the clay. Add water very slowly, drip by drip, and stir until you've bound everything together. The mixture should be moist, not dripping wet.

4 Knead the mixture with your hands. Take a handful of the mixture, and shape it into a ball—around the size of a golf ball. Use the rest of the mixture to make more balls.

5 Leave your seedballs to dry for a day or two. Then go to your chosen location, and . . . THROW! If they land on concrete or rock, don't worry—the seeds have everything they need to grow in the ball. Don't worry about watering either—nature will take care of that.

6 Return in a few weeks to check on your instant garden. Keep visiting to see it in full bloom.

IMPORTANT!

Make sure that you don't throw seedballs onto other people's property if you don't have their permission first. But if you think your neighbor, school, or local business has a patch of ground that could do with livening up, find out who's in charge and see if they'll play ball—"seedball," that is . . .

DONE! | DATE COMPLETED

25 MAKE AN OUTDOOR PHOTO BOOTH

Don't be shy! Step right up! Everyone loves taking silly pictures. This simple booth will allow you and your friends to have hours of fun and lots of memorable snaps.

YOU WILL NEED:

- Large picture frame
- Fishing line
- A sturdy tree branch
- Dress-up clothes or props
- Cell phone or camera

1 Find a large picture frame. It needs to be at least big enough to fit your head into. If you don't have something at home, hunt one down in a local thrift store.

2 Remove the backing and everything in the frame. You might need an adult to help you to do this. Repaint or decorate the frame if you want to.

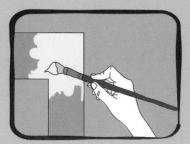

3 Find a tree with a sturdy branch in a nice setting for a photo. Ask an adult to help you to hang the frame from the branch with fishing line. You could also hang it from a post or hook.

4 Try out different heights and positions, for example, an oval frame might be nice on its side so that two people can fit into it. Make sure the frame isn't too high to reach! It needs to be at eye level.

5 Put a few props or an entire dress-up box on the ground near the frame.

6 Invite your friends over, ask them to stand behind the frame, and take their portrait! Encourage them to get inventive with the props.

DONE! DATE COMPLETED

26 CLIMB A TREE

The world looks different from up here! Climb a tree and see everything from a new perspective. It's a pretty good hiding place too! Be sure to choose a dry day, as wet weather will make it much harder to climb.

1 Wear sturdy footwear to help you grip onto the bark, and long sleeves and pants to protect you from scrapes and scratches. Find a big, sturdy tree with plenty of strong branches at regular intervals. Before climbing, do a few stretches to warm up.

2 Now stretch up to reach the first branch. Choose a branch that is at least as thick as your arm. Hold on to the branch tightly, test it to make sure that it will take your weight, and pull yourself up the trunk. As you climb up farther, look for knots, bulges, crevices, and smaller branches to use as footholds.

3 Only climb up as far as you feel comfortable and safe. You can always climb higher next time! Take time to enjoy your view. Look around for animals living in the tree. Climb back down very carefully when you're ready to.

SAFETY FIRST!
Don't go too high up. Always take an adult with you. You might need help getting up or down the tree.

DONE! DATE COMPLETED

CLOUD SHAPING 27

It's been said that clouds are the sky's imagination. Why not catch a little of its creative magic and try some cloud shaping?

1 Lie down on your back and stare into the sky. Watch the clouds drift by.

2 Let your mind wander. What do you see? Are there castles, horses, monsters . . .? Keep looking until you see something. Relax and just "be."

3 Now look at the blue spaces between the clouds. Pictures lie hidden there too.

TOP TIP
Cloud pictures don't just appear in blue summer skies. Try cloud shaping at sunrise and sunset and during a storm too.

DONE!   DATE COMPLETED

28 BUILD A BUCKET POND

You don't need a big space for a simple outdoor pond. You don't even need to dig a hole! Try this simple project, and wait for the wildlife to visit.

YOU WILL NEED:

- Watertight container, for example, an old bucket or baby bath
- Washed sand
- Washed pebbles
- Washed larger rocks and stones
- Terra-cotta flowerpots
- Water plants (available from garden centers—ask advice on the best ones to buy to oxygenate your pond)
- Rain water

1 Find a container. You can use anything—from an old bucket or old-fashioned bathtub to an old baby bath or storage box—as long as it is watertight. It shouldn't be too deep so that creatures can get up to it easily. Wash it out thoroughly.

2 Pour washed sand into the bottom of your container until you've covered the base. Scatter pebbles over the sand. This will give the insects somewhere to bury and hide.

3 Put your flowerpots in upside down, then add the bigger rocks and stones. These will provide shelter for the wildlife.

4 Add some water plants. Check with the garden center when you buy them that you're including good oxygenators.

5 Put in a shady spot so it doesn't overheat in the sun. Pile stones around the edge to help frogs and other creatures climb up. Place other plants nearby.

6 Fill up with rainwater. Don't use tap water—it has chemicals in it that might harm your pond life. Then just wait for your visitors!

DONE!

DATE COMPLETED

29 HAVE A WATER CUP RACE

If you don't feel like getting soaked through with yet another water fight, use your water pistols for a cup race instead. All you need are plastic cups and string. Load . . . aim . . . go!

1 Ask an adult to help you make holes in the bottom of some plastic cups.

2 Set up a string line for each player by tying one end of each string to a post or a tree. Thread a cup onto the string before tying the other end. Make sure that each player's string is the same length—no cheating!

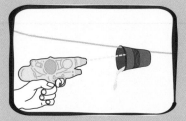

3 Pull the cups to equal starting positions. Place the bucket of water between each starting string line. Load your guns, and race your way to the finishing line!

WHY NOT?
Practice on your own using a stopwatch. What's your best time?

DONE! DATE COMPLETED

INVITE YOUR FRIENDS TO A PICNIC

What better way to spend a gloriously sunny afternoon than with friends on a picnic? Plan ahead so you don't forget anything!

1 Decide on a lovely picnic spot—it might be in your local park, on the beach, or in your own garden. Then write invitations to your friends. Don't forget to say where, when, and what to bring.

2 Make a list of who's coming and the food to prepare. Think carefully about what everyone likes to eat. Sandwiches or wraps and fruit are good starting points. List items that your friends have promised to bring so that you can work out whether there will be enough to go around. An adult can help you to do this as well as to go shopping.

3 Set out with at least one friend, and make sure that an adult knows where you're going. Get there a little early so you're there before your other guests. Lay out the picnic blanket, eat, relax, talk, and throw a Frisbee! Don't forget to take all of your trash home with you.

WHY NOT?
Try a winter picnic with flasks of hot chocolate or soup. Wrap up warm, and take blankets to cozy up in!

DONE!

DATE COMPLETED

31 MAKE A STICK FAMILY

When you're next in the park or the woods, try making your very own stick family. Add a few googly eyes and some other bits and pieces, and they'll really come to life.

YOU WILL NEED:

- Sticks (found on the ground)
- Googly eyes
- Marker pens
- Bits of fabric
- Scissors
- Glue
- Thread or pipe cleaners

1 Pick out your favorite sticks, and decide which to use for the bodies. Is there a cute little one for "baby"? Use thread or pipe cleaners to tie on smaller twigs for arms and legs.

2 Stick on googly eyes. Knobbly bits might suggest open mouths or lips. You can also use the marker pens to draw on some facial features.

3 Wrap pieces of fabric around them for clothes. A ribbon tied under a "chin" makes for a good bow tie.

DONE!   DATE COMPLETED

FEED THE BIRDS | 32

When food is hard to find in the winter, a peanut butter feeder will help to feed the local birds. If possible, hang it within view of your bedroom window.

1 Cut a length of string and tie it securely to the top of the pinecone.

2 Put the birdseed and any extras, such as sunflower seeds, corn, or nuts, into a bowl. Spread peanut butter all over the cone with a knife or spoon.

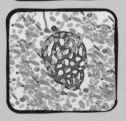

3 Dip the sticky cone into your bowl of seed. Roll it around until the peanut butter is completely covered with seed.

YOU WILL NEED:

- Pinecone
- Birdseed
- Peanut butter
- String
- Scissors
- Butter knife
- Thread or pipe cleaners

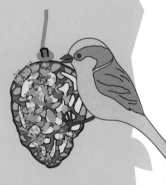

4 Ask an adult to help you to hang it from a tree branch or up high. Make sure that animals that like to eat birds can't reach it. Try to identify your visitors by looking them up in a bird-spotting guide or on the Internet.

DONE!   DATE COMPLETED

33 PLAY ELBOW TAG

You've probably played tag, but have you played this version? It's quite a challenge and best with a big group of friends in a large space.

YOU WILL NEED:

- A group of friends (at least 8, but the more the better!)
- Large area to run around in

1 Split into pairs. If there's anyone left over, have one group of three. Stand in your pairs with your elbows linked. Spread out in the play area.

2 Choose one pair to unlink elbows and become "It" and the Runner. Whoever is "It" chases the Runner. If the Runner is caught, he or she is tagged and will become "It." In turn, "It" will become the Runner.

3 To escape "It," the Runner can link elbows with one of the pairs to make a threesome. He or she is now safe. But the person at the other end of the threesome is now the Runner.

4 "It" must chase the new Runner. The new Runner can link onto a pair to pass on the role, but it must be a different pair from the one they were in before.

5 At any point, if "It" tags the Runner, the roles reverse. Play until you're all so exhausted that you fall down in a big heap!

WHY NOT?
Change the rules a little. You could speed-walk or hop instead of run.

DONE!   DATE COMPLETED

34 MAKE BARK AND LEAF RUBBINGS

Using paper and crayons, take rubbings of bark textures and leaf patterns, and start your own collection. Mount them in a scrapbook and use the Internet or a guide to identify them.

1 Place a piece of paper on the bark of a tree, and hold it in place with one hand. Rub a crayon smoothly across it, keeping all the strokes in one direction using the side of the crayon. The pattern of the bark and its ridges will be transferred to your paper.

2 Choose a leaf. It should be dry. Leaves that have lots of veins and ribs on them work best.

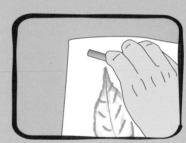

3 Place your leaf on a firm surface and put a strong piece of paper over it. Use your crayon in the same way that you did for the bark rubbing—keeping all the strokes in the same direction. One side of your leaf will be smoother than the other. Try rubbing both sides.

DONE!   DATE COMPLETED

THROW PAPER-PLATE FRISBEES

If you don't own a Frisbee, don't worry—it's very easy to make one with a couple of paper plates. So, how far can you throw it?

YOU WILL NEED:

- 2 paper plates
- Scissors
- Adhesive tape
- Marker pens

1 Cover one side of each plate with adhesive tape. Place the plates right side up, as if you're going to put food on them. Cover them with strips of adhesive tape, letting them overlap the edges.

2 Trim around the outer edge of each plate to remove the extra tape. Make a hole in the center of one of the plates. Use a protractor or draw around a lid or a saucer to get a perfect circle. Pierce the center of the circle with scissors to cut it out. Now cut a hole in the other plate in the same way.

3 Turn the plates over and decorate with marker pens. Now cover the decorated sides of your plates with tape. Let the tape hang over the sides, and trim it on one plate as before. Leave the overhanging tape on the other plate and use it to join the two plates together. Now you're ready to play!

DONE! | DATE COMPLETED

36 SEND A SEMAPHORE

The semaphore flag system was designed more than 150 years ago, and it is still used today. Make yourself a semaphore flag and try signaling a message to your friends from the other side of a football field (or from the bottom of your garden).

YOU WILL NEED:

- 2 sheets of thick yellow paper
- 2 sheets of thick red paper
- Paper glue
- Ruler
- Pencil
- 2 dowels or flower sticks
- Adhesive tape
- Notebook and pen (for the person receiving your signals)

1 Draw a diagonal line from the top right-hand corner to the bottom left-hand corner of each yellow sheet of paper. Cut along the lines. Glue each triangle onto the backs and fronts of the red papers, making sure that the red triangles are always at the top.

2 Place the adhesive tape along the left-hand edge of each flag, half on the paper, half off.

3 Place the dowel over the tape, lining it up with the top of the flag. Flip over the flag and pull the tape tight, rolling the paper around the dowel as you go. Press hard to make sure that the tape sticks to the dowel and the paper.

4 Time to try some semaphore! Use the alphabet opposite to practice a few words that you'd like to signal. Lend this book to your friends to read your signals. You can stand as far away from them as you like as long as they can still see your bright flags!

THE SEMAPHORE ALPHABET

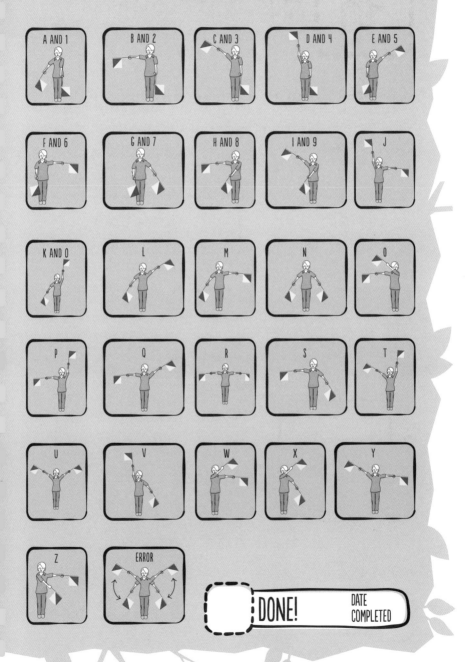

37 SKIP YOURSELF FIT

Skipping is a great workout. It's lots of fun too! If you haven't done it for a while, build up slowly.

1 Warm up gently with a slow Double Hop. This is when you skip with your feet together, turning the rope slowly. Jump twice between each rope turn. Try 10 of these.

2 Next, do the Shuffle. This is when you put one foot in front of the other and switch feet as you skip. Jump twice between each rope swing. If you feel ready, try to speed it up with just one jump between each rope swing. Do 10 of these.

3 Now for the High Knee. Pick up one knee at a time while you skip. Again, start off by jumping twice between each rope swing. When you're ready, jump just once, as if you're running with your knees up high. Do 10 of these.

4 Time to cool down with some knee tucks. Take one knee in both hands and pull it up to your chest. Do the same with the other knee. Do again on both sides. If you're tired, go and rest. If you feel like you can do more, start back at step 1. Maybe try 15 of each this time instead of 10?

DONE! DATE COMPLETED

MAKE DRIP CASTLES

You don't have to go to the beach to build these wild, magical towers—a sandbox will work just great!

YOU WILL NEED:

- A sandy beach or a tray of sand in your outdoor space
- A bucket

1 Prepare a solid base. If you're on the beach, pile up wet sand and flatten it. If you're at home, you could just work on a paving stone.

2 Half fill your bucket with sand. Then fill to the top with water. Stir with your hand to get a gooey mix.

3 Collect a handful of your gooey sand mixture. Point your sand-filled hand thumb down. Then let some of the goo drip through your fingers. As the sand drips, it will build up into a stalactite structure.

4 Keep dripping, moving your hand up and away from the tower as it gets taller. Group lots together, or build towers on top of towers to create one big one. Arrange in a circle for a ring of mountain peaks, or make a castle!

DONE!   DATE COMPLETED

39 LAY A STICK TRAIL

Are you a good trailblazer? Head for the local woodland or park, and lay a trail for your friends to follow and find you. If there's a big group of you, split into Trailblazers and Trackers. The Trailblazers set the trail for the Trackers.

YOU WILL NEED:

- Bucket
- Sticks, stones, and other natural objects (found on the ground)
- A few friends

1 Gather together sticks, stones, pinecones, feathers, leaves, and any other natural objects you can find, and put them in your bucket. Don't pick anything from the trees—there will be plenty on the ground.

2 Decide on where your track will start and finish, and lay trails along the route. You can make up your own symbols, or use some of the examples on the opposite page.

3 Now it's time for your friends to track you down. Use a few sticks to show them what to look out for and what your symbols mean. Ask them to count to 100 while you race to the end of your trail and hide. Can they follow your trail to find you?

SAFETY FIRST

Always tell your parents where you are going.

GO STRAIGHT ON

TURN LEFT

TURN RIGHT

WRONG WAY

3 STEPS TO THE RIGHT

FOLLOW THE STREAM

GO OVER AN OBSTACLE

DONE!   DATE COMPLETED

40 PLAY BEANBAG LADDER TOSS

Are you better at throwing overarm or underarm? Can you throw blind? Practice your aim using just a step ladder, sheets of paper, colored markers, and beanbags.

1 Write the scores onto different sheets of paper with colored markers. You will need to write the scores: 10, 20, 30 (×2), 40, and 50. Make sure you draw the numbers big and bold so that you can see them easily.

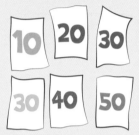

2 Ask an adult to put up a step ladder in a large space outside. Tape the score papers onto the steps, with one of the 30 points sheets hanging from the bottom step, and then in ascending order (10, 20, 30, 40, 50) as you travel up the steps. Ask an adult to hold the ladder for you, and to help you to tape the scores onto the higher steps.

3 Now it's time to play! Either take turns with friends or play solo, trying to beat your best score each time. Your aim is to throw the beanbags between the steps of the ladder and win the number of points hanging above that hole. If your beanbag lands on a step, you lose 5 points.

DONE! DATE COMPLETED

MAKE A DAISY CHAIN

Flower power! Garlands, crowns, necklaces, bracelets, rings . . . you can make them all with these cute little flowers.

1 Find a daisy patch. Pick a few flowers with really long stems.

2 Use your thumbnail to carve a small slit into one daisy stem. (It's best to do this at the thickest part of the stem.)

3 Thread another daisy through the slit. Then make a slit in the stem of that daisy. Thread a daisy through that, and so on. Keep on going until your chain is the right length for your daisy jewelry.

4 To finish off, just make a slit in the last stem and thread the first daisy back through it. Wear your daisies with pride!

DONE!   DATE COMPLETED

LAUNCH A TOY PARACHUTE

Have you ever dreamed of making a parachute jump? Maybe you should let your toy action figure have a go first . . .

YOU WILL NEED:

- 10-inch square piece of lightweight fabric
- Scissors
- A button with 4 holes
- Two lengths of 36-inch thread
- Small plastic action figure

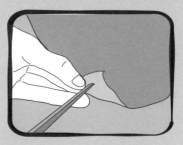

1 Fold over one corner of the fabric and snip a small hole with the scissors. Repeat on the other three sides.

2 Take one of your threads. Tie one end to the corner of the fabric.

3 Take the other end of the thread through one button hole then through the diagonally opposite button hole.

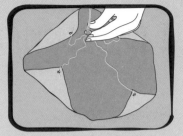

4 Pull the thread until the button is in the middle and tie the loose end to the opposite corner of the fabric. Repeat with the other thread and corners.

5 Hold the threads from the top of the button. Slide the button down about two-thirds of the thread and tie a knot.

6 Tie the action figure to the end of the parachute. You're now ready for a test flight. Launch the parachute by throwing it in the air. Or drop it from a height (such as a wall, tree, or chair) with the help of an adult.

DONE!   DATE COMPLETED

43 CARVE A HALLOWEEN PUMPKIN

It's traditional to have a pumpkin lantern on your porch at Halloween. How scary can you make yours?

1 Ask an adult to cut off the crown (top) of the pumpkin with a sharp, serrated knife. Put the top to one side.

2 Scoop out the pumpkin flesh, pulp, and seeds with a spoon. (If you wash and dry the seeds, you can use them later to make art or jewelry.)

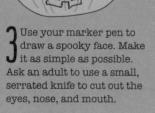

3 Use your marker pen to draw a spooky face. Make it as simple as possible. Ask an adult to use a small, serrated knife to cut out the eyes, nose, and mouth.

4 Put a tea light in the bottom of your pumpkin to light after dark. Pop on the lid, place on your doorstep, and ward away all evil!

DONE! DATE COMPLETED

MAKE A STRING TELEPHONE

The way that a string telephone works isn't so different from how an old-fashioned telephone worked, except that string is used instead of an electric current. Try different lengths of string to see how far away it will work.

YOU WILL NEED:

- 2 paper cups
- Non-stretchable thread (for example, kite string or fishing line)
- Measuring tape or ruler
- Sewing needle
- A friend

HOW DOES IT WORK?

When you talk into your cup, the bottom vibrates back and forth with sound waves. The vibrations travel along the string and are converted back into sound waves at the other end so your friend can hear what you said. Sound waves travel better through solids (such as your cup and string) than through air, letting you hear sounds that are much farther away.

1 Cut a long length of string between 65–100 feet. Ask an adult to help you make holes in the bottom of your cups with a sewing needle. Thread the string through each cup and tie a knot at each end, inside the cups.

2 Take one of the cups each, and spread apart until the string is tight. One of you should talk into the cup while the other one listens. Can you hear what the other person is saying?

DONE!

DATE COMPLETED

45 BUILD A BOTTLE TOWER GARDEN

You don't need a big garden to grow vegetables and flowers. In fact, all you need to make this garden is a trellised wall or fence and lots of large plastic bottles!

YOU WILL NEED:

- Large plastic bottles with screw tops (2-liter soda bottles are perfect)
- Scissors
- An adult with a drill and a sharp knife
- Compost
- Handful of clean sand
- Seeds, seedlings, or small plants
- A trellised wall, fence, or freestanding trellis
- Garden twine
- Watering can

1 Clean the bottles and remove any labels. Ask an adult to help you to cut off the bottoms with a pair of sharp scissors.

2 Keep the lid on your first bottle. Ask an adult to help you make a small drainage hole at the top, at the bottle neck. Make another hole on the opposite side.

3 Fill the bottle with potting compost, leaving 1 inch at the top of the tower. Stand the bottle on the ground, lid down, next to the fence or wall to make the bottom of the tower.

4 Take the lid off your second bottle and fill it with compost. Place it on top of the first bottle. Use garden twine to secure the bottles to your fence or trellis.

5 Add a third, fourth, and even fifth bottle to your tower in the same way. The sixth bottle will be the funnel. It should have no soil and no lid. Cut it down a little more than the others and put it into the top bottle.

6 Bottle number 7 needs its lid. Ask an adult to drill a very small hole into the lid. Add a handful of sand to the bottle to filter the water. This is your filling-up bottle, which drops water through all of the other bottles.

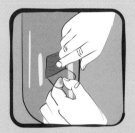

7 Ask an adult to make windows in each bottle by cutting 3 lines into the plastic with a sharp knife. Pull down a rectangle of plastic. Push a hole into the compost and plant a seed, seedling, or small plant inside.

8 Keep your filling-up bottle well watered, and watch your garden grow!

DONE!

DATE COMPLETED

46 MAKE SUN PRINTS

Get creative with sun print papers. Special chemicals in the papers react to sunlight and help you to create awesome shadow prints. They're so cool, you'll want to hang them in your room!

YOU WILL NEED:

- Sun print paper (available from toy stores and on the Internet)
- Interesting-shaped objects, for example, toys, leaves, keys, etc.
- Tray
- Large plastic bowl of clean water
- Paper towels
- A sunny spot outdoors

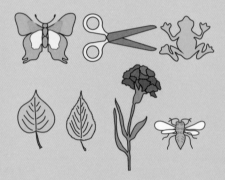

1 Find some fun-shaped objects. Small toys, plastic insects, leaves, keys, scissors, and flowers all work well.

2 Choose a shady spot, or do this part indoors, away from the window. Place a couple of sheets of sun print paper onto the tray. Make sure they don't overlap. Arrange your objects onto the papers.

3 Carry the tray to a sunny spot, taking care not to move the objects out of place. Leave the tray in the sunshine for 2 to 5 minutes. (If it's a little cloudy, leave for up to 20 minutes.)

4 Take a bowl of clean water out to the tray. When the sun paper has faded to white, take the objects off. Put the paper into the bowl. Leave it in the water for a few minutes. This is where the magic happens—the shapes of your objects will become white, and the faded blue background will become a dark blue color.

5 Take your sun prints out of the water and rest them on some paper towels to dry. Impressed? Why not hang them in your room?

DONE!   DATE COMPLETED

47 PLAY POOH STICKS

You can thank Pooh Bear for the invention of this super simple game. Pooh played it on a warm, sunny day with his friends. Play it with yours the next time you cross a bridge over a stream.

1 Each find a stick. Look at each other's sticks, and agree whose is whose. You could even tie a piece of different-colored string to each stick to remind you which is yours.

2 Gather on the side of the bridge where the stream runs in (upstream). Stand side by side, holding your stick at arms length over the stream.

3 Ready, Steady, GO! Drop your sticks at the same time.

4 Run to the other side of the bridge (downstream). Whoever's stick appears first wins!

DONE! DATE COMPLETED

GO SLEDDING

 48

There's nothing like zooming down the slopes on a sled, but make sure you do it safely. Wheee!

1 Wrap up warm, with a waterproof coat, pants, gloves, hat, and boots. Wear lots of layers underneath to keep toasty and dry, but don't wear a scarf. Wear lip balm, and put some in your pocket to reapply. Put on your helmet.

2 Choose a good sledding hill: not too steep with a long flat area at the bottom, away from any roads and ponds, is perfect. It should be snowy rather than icy and free of obstacles such as rocks or trees.

3 Put your sled on the top of the hill. Sit on it facing forward, with your arms and legs inside the sled, not dangling over the sides. Push off with your hands, and hold on tightly to the sides. If you fall off, move out of the way of your sled and any other sledders. If you can't stop, roll off the sled and get out of the way. GERONIMO! Time to go again? Walk back up the side of the hill, leaving the middle open for other sledders.

SAFETY FIRST
Always take an adult with you. Make sure that your sled can brake and steer. Practice braking before taking your sled on a hill, and only sled in the daytime.

DONE!   DATE COMPLETED

49 GROW A BAG OF STRAWBERRIES

Instead of taking your shopping bag to the grocery store to buy strawberries, fill it with compost and grow them instead! They're delicious with cream when they're ripe.

YOU WILL NEED:

- A sturdy reusable shopping bag
- 8 strawberry plants
- 1 bag of potting compost
- Scissors
- Broken egg shells
- Petroleum jelly

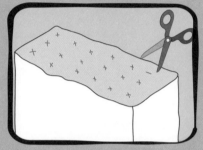

1 Ask an adult to help you cut drainage holes in the bottom of your shopping bag with the scissors. It's easiest to snip a hole, and then cut a cross shape.

2 Cut a horizontal slit about 5 cm across in the middle of the bag's front and back. Then cut two slits in the middle of each side of the bag.

3 Put your bag in a sunny, sheltered spot. It needs to be at least 1 foot above the ground, so you might want to rest it on a crate or small table. This will allow the plants to hang down without touching the ground.

4 Fill your bag with potting compost up to the level of the slits. Put 6 strawberry plants inside. Working from the inside, poke the leaves and crown (the part where the stems of the leaves meet in the middle) of each plant carefully through each slit. Spread the roots out in the bag.

5 Fill the bag almost to the top with the potting compost, and plant your remaining 2 plants at the top. Make sure that their roots are completely covered. Sprinkle broken eggshells onto the soil at the top (eggshells add calcium to your fertilizer) and smear petroleum jelly onto the sides of the bag to keep snails and slugs away.

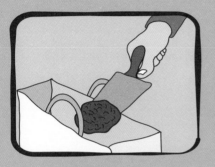

6 Water until the compost is evenly moist. Keep well watered. Every few days, rotate your bag so that all the plants get the same amount of sunshine. Then just wait for your strawberries to appear! After flowering, you should get ripe berries in just a couple of weeks. Don't be impatient—wait until they're red all over before picking the fruit.

DONE!   DATE COMPLETED

50 CREATE A SAND PALACE

Build a showstopping sandcastle fit for a king or queen. You'll need lots of wet sand and a bucketful of imagination!

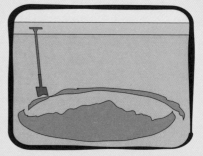

1 Find a good spot on the beach just above the tide line (where the dark sand becomes lighter). Use a long shovel to dig a circle in the sand, piling the sand up into the middle to make a hill. Don't forget to bend your knees!

2 Stamp the top of your hill into a volcano crater shape. Pour water into your crater. Use your feet to push down the sand. This will be the foundation for your sand palace.

3 Now put your dustbin on top. Fill it three-fourths full with sand. Pour in a few buckets of water, and press down the sand with your hands or a bucket. Add more sand and water. Keep going until it is full.

4 Add a slightly smaller bottomless container on top. Add sand until it's three-fourths full. Add water and push down, as in step 2. Continue to add and fill the smaller containers on top of one another.

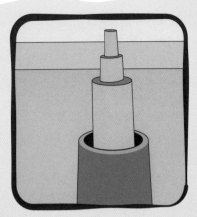

5 Carefully pat the sides of the top container, and pull it off the top tower very slowly. Release all your containers from the top down.

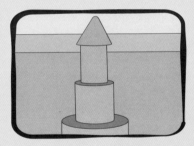

6 Add a turret. Fill the funnel with very wet sand, and put it on your top tower. Smooth the sand down. A makeup brush or spatula is good for this. You can add wet sand to finish off edges too.

7 And now for the detail. Always start carving from the top down so that the sand falls away from your finished areas. Keep the sand wet with your spray bottle. Join towers with spiraling ramps, using craft sticks to make steps. Cut archways, doorways, and windows . . . and don't forget to put flags on the top!

DONE!   DATE COMPLETED

51 FORECAST THE WEATHER WITH A PINECONE

Pinecones naturally close when it is wet and open up when it is dry, so they are great weather indicators. Use one to make your very own weather-predicting hygroscope!

1 Cut off the top of a flexible straw at the top where it bends.

2 Position the tip of the straw on top of an open scale of the pinecone. Glue into place.

3 Put your pinecone onto a window ledge. When the air is humid, the scales of the pinecone will close and the straw will rise. This means that it is likely to rain. When it is sunny, the scales open up and the straw bends down.

WET

DRY

DONE! DATE COMPLETED

HAVE A TREASURE HUNT

Challenge friends and family to a treasure hunt around the backyard or in your local park. Don't forget to hide the "treasure" at the last clue!

YOU WILL NEED:

- 10–15 luggage labels with string
- Pen
- Adhesive tape
- Small prizes, for example, wrapped candy (optional)
- Treasure prize

CLUES—APPLE TREE, BIKE, FRONT DOOR, BBQ, BACK DOOR, ROSE BUSH, BIRD FEEDER, SWING, GARDEN TABLE, PINE TREE
TREASURE—IN THE SHED

I GET HOT AND COOK SAUSAGES

1 Decide on where you're going to hide the treasure, how many clues there will be (10–15 works well), and where you're going to tie them. Write a list to help you remember.

2 Write the clues on the luggage labels. They might be pictures, e.g., draw an apple if the next clue can be found on the apple tree; descriptions, e.g., "I get hot and cook sausages" for the BBQ; or rhymes, e.g., "On me you can speed like a bird in the sky, my two wheels will make you fly!" for your bike.

3 If you want to, you could tape small prizes to the luggage labels, such as wrapped candies. Tie the clues around the garden, always tying them to the next clue rather than the answer. Then hide the treasure.

4 Invite friends and family to hunt for the clues, removing them as they go—who will find the treasure first? You can help them if they get stuck, and if you're feeling super generous, have small consolation prizes for the losers.

DONE!   DATE COMPLETED

53 THREAD A FLOWER GARLAND

In Hawaii, a flower garland is called a lei and is used to welcome visitors. Why not make your own to greet your friends?

YOU WILL NEED:

- Fresh flowers (with big receptacles—the thicker green part at the top of the stem)
- Scissors
- Strong thread
- Thick darning needle

1 Pick or buy the flowers that you'd like to use. If you're picking, check with the person who planted them first! You'll need about 40 flower heads for a full garland.

2 Cut the flower buds from the stem by snipping them at the bottom of the receptacle. Set the flowers aside, making sure that you don't crush the petals.

3 Measure a double length of thread around your neck to decide on the length of the garland. Add about 10 inches for tying off. Thread the needle and knot the ends.

4 Divide your flowers into two equal piles. For the first half, insert the needle through the flower from head to stem.

5 For the second half, insert the needle the other way around—from the stem through to the flower.

6 Push the flowers together on the thread. Then tie the garland into a circle by knotting the ends. Now greet your friends with a lei!

TOP TIP
Alternate the type and color of flowers in the garland for a burst of color.

DONE!

DATE COMPLETED

54 RIDE THE WAVES

If you've never been surfing, why not start with a boogie (or body) board? Just lie on top of the board and ride a wave to the beach. Surf's up!

YOU WILL NEED:

- Waves
- Sunblock
- Bodyboard
- Leash
- Wetsuit (it needs to fit snugly but still allow movement)
- Booties
- Fins
  (A wetsuit, booties, and fins can all be hired with a body board)

1 Watch someone else bodyboard first to get the idea. Then practice on the beach, using your feet and arms to paddle. This will give you a nice warm up, too.

2 Now it's time to get into the water! Make sure you're wearing your leash. Lie flat on your belly holding the side of the board with your hands. Keep your shoulders parallel to your hands, with your elbows bent, resting close to the outer edge of the board. Kick your feet, keeping them underwater.

SAFETY FIRST!

The beach can be very dangerous if you're not careful. Always take an adult with you, and do not try to boogie board unless you are a good swimmer. Always make sure that you don't go too far out so that you don't get caught in a strong ocean current.

3 Kick and paddle to where the waves are breaking. Choose the wave you want to ride, starting with a small one. A few seconds before the wave starts to break, point the nose of your board toward the beach.

4 Just as the wave reaches you, push off toward the shore. Let the board take your weight and lean up on your elbows with your head up and your back arched.

5 If you've caught the wave, it'll take you all the way to the beach. Was that fun? Time to go back in!

TOP TIP

Make sure that you have the right size board. They range from 36 to 46 inches long. Stand the board upright. It should come up to your belly button, or about 1 inch on either side of it. E.g., if you're 4 feet tall, then you're 48 inches tall, so your body board would be 36 inches long.

DON'T PANIC!

If you fall off your board, don't worry—pull on your leash until you get hold of it again. Your board will keep you afloat.

DONE!   DATE COMPLETED

55 MAKE A BALLOON ROCKET

Real rockets need fuel to launch them into space, but you can send yours whizzing across the garden using just escaping air!

YOU WILL NEED:

- Balloon
- String
- Plastic drinking straw
- Masking tape
- 2 posts, trees, or hooks
  (at least 9 feet apart)

1 Tie one end of the string to a post or tree. Thread the loose end of the string through the straw. Pull the string tight before fixing it to the other post.

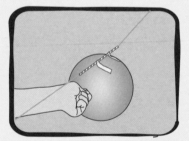

2 Blow up the balloon, but don't tie it off. Pinch the end and don't let go! Tape the balloon to the straw.

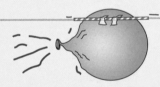

3 Pull the straw and balloon to one end of the string. Let go for blastoff! How quickly can it get to the end of the string?

DONE!   DATE COMPLETED

MAKE MUD FACES

After a rain shower, there's plenty of mud around.
It's the perfect time to create a mud face. Will it be
a beast or a beauty? A friend or a foe?

1 Dig up some mud and put it in a bucket. The stickier the mud is, the better. Add water to make it stickier if you need to.

2 Make a mud ball in your hands, and squash it onto the tree trunk, shaping it into a face.

3 Use natural materials to add features like eyes, teeth, a mouth, a nose, hair, and horns. Moss and fern leaves are perfect for shaggy hair, and pinecones are great for noses, horns, fangs, and eyes.

4 Name your beast, sprite, monster, or goddess, and leave it for someone else to find. When you go back, maybe another face will have appeared!

DONE!   DATE COMPLETED

57 MAKE TWINKLING LANTERNS

The flickering light of a lantern is all you need to enjoy your outdoor space after sundown. If you decorate it with magical creatures and tell imaginative stories, who knows what'll happen!

YOU WILL NEED:

- Old jelly jar (or several)
- Acrylic paint pens
- 20 inches thin garden wire
- Beads
- Play sand
- Container with lid
- Food coloring
- Tea light (if possible, use Citronella to ward off mosquitoes and other biting insects)

1 Decorate your jelly jar with acrylic paint pens. You could draw patterns and shapes or fairies, dragons, and other magical creatures. Leave to dry.

2 Now make the handle. Bend a loop at one end of the garden wire. Thread your beads from the other side until half the wire is covered.

3 Wrap the leftover wire around the neck of the jelly jar, twisting the end to secure it.

4 Bend the beaded wire over the jelly jar. Undo the loop you made in step 2, and thread this wire through the neck wire. Twist to secure, and tuck in any ends.

5 Take the lid off your container and put in a couple of spoonfuls of sand. Add a few drops of food coloring. Replace the lid and secure tightly. Shake for a minute.

6 Pour the sand into the bottom of your jelly jar and add in a tea light. Hang your lantern up outside, ask an adult to help you light it up at twilight or use battery-operated tea lights. What sort of magic can you make happen?

DONE!

DATE COMPLETED

[58] PLAY HOPSCOTCH

It's thought this game began in ancient Roman times. Soldiers ran over courses 100 feet long in full armor to improve their footwork. Don't worry—yours can be much shorter, and you can wear anything you like!

YOU WILL NEED:

- Chalk (or stone that leaves marks on a sidewalk)
- A small stone
- Sidewalk or area you can chalk on
- Any number of players— you can do this solo too

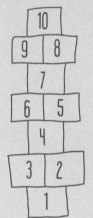

1 Draw a hopscotch course on the ground. Make sure the squares are big enough to fit one hopping foot!

2 Throw a stone to land on square 1. It mustn't bounce out or touch the border! If you don't get within the lines, you lose your turn and pass the stone to the next player.

3 If your stone lands in the first square, you can start your hopscotch. Hop over the first square, planting both feet on squares 2 and 3. Then hopscotch your way to number 10, hopping in single squares with one foot, and planting both feet on the side-by-side squares.

4 When you reach number 10, turn around on one foot and go back again. Don't forget to hop over square 1! If at any point you step on a line or lose balance, it's the next person's turn.

5 Now its time to throw your stone into square number 2. This time, you'll need to hop into squares 1, 3, and 4 before you plant both feet onto 5 and 6. Keep throwing your stone into the squares in order, and hopscotch your way through the course. You can just count up to 10, or do the countdown (from 9 to 1), too. Always hop over the squares with stones!

6 If you're really good, you'll finish the course before the next person even has a chance to take a turn, and you WIN! But it's more likely that you'll take turns until one person has finished.

WHY NOT?
Change the shape of the hopscotch course! You could try a spiral shape, or even try separating the boxes and jumping between them!

DON'T FORGET
to wash away your course at the end of the game.

DONE! DATE COMPLETED

59 SAIL A LEAF BOAT

If you happen to be near a pond, stream, or lake, you can launch your leaf boat there. An upturned trash-can lid or wheelbarrow full of water will do just as well!

1 Collect your materials. You will need a "seaworthy" piece of bark, flat and broad enough to form the hull (the base) of your boat. If there's no bark on the ground, you could peel it away from a fallen, rotting tree trunk.

2 The bark may already have a hole in it, made by insect larvae. If not, make a small hole with a twig. (It helps if the bark is wet and softened.) Make the hole as central as possible, and push a twig into it, making sure it fits snugly. This will be your mast.

3 Thread a big leaf or series of leaves onto the stick for a sail. Find some water and launch your boat!

DONE! DATE COMPLETED

WHY NOT?
Add a passenger! Find a small pebble or flower head. Place it on the hull or on top of the mast, as if in a crow's nest. Will it stay aboard?

TAKE LAVENDER CUTTINGS

60

Lavender smells lovely in your garden or on a windowsill. If you have a plant already, take cuttings in the summer, and you'll have more plants in the spring.

1 Choose a plant that is nice and healthy, with no pests or diseases. Look for a straight, healthy stem without any flower buds. Make sure that the stem is hard, not soft, and carefully cut it off with scissors. Remove the lower leaves so that the cutting has a bare stem.

2 Fill your pot with potting compost (first, mix it with grit if you have some). Push your cuttings into the side of the pot between the pot and the compost.

3 Water well and cover the pot with a plastic bag to keep it humid. Put it in a warm, shady place. Once the rooting has started, remove the plastic bag. When your cuttings are well rooted, move them into their own pots.

DONE! DATE COMPLETED

61 MAKE AND PLAY PEBBLE DOMINOES

It's so tempting to collect those lovely smooth, flat stones on the beach or in the backyard. But what do you do with them? With a little bit of paint and a steady hand, you can turn them into dominoes. This game has been popular since ancient times—a set was found in Tutankhamen's tomb!

YOU WILL NEED:

- 28 smooth, flat stones
- White paint pen (or acrylic paint, a small brush and a steady hand)

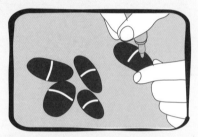

1 Collect 28 smooth, flat stones. Wash them to remove any sand or soil and paint a white line across the center of each.

DOMINO PIECE GUIDE

2 Then, on either side of the lines, mark with two sets of dots in every combination from zero to six. Use this guide to make sure that you don't miss any.

3 When the paint is dry, play with your dominoes on the lawn or at an outdoor table. You need at least one other player. First, place the dominos facedown (with no dots showing) and shuffle them around. This is the boneyard. (This is because dominoes were originally made out of bone, or ivory. Yuck!)

4 Each player takes 7 dominoes. The players should see their own dominoes, but not the other players'. No peeking! Decide who starts by each picking up a domino from the boneyard. The player with the highest number of dots goes first.

5 Lay the first domino. The next player places one of his or her dominoes at one end of the first domino by matching the number of dots. If he or she can't go, then he or she should pick up a new pebble from the boneyard.

6 The game continues with each player matching one end of the domino chain in turn. If a double is laid, set the pebble vertically rather than horizontally. Every time you can't go, pick up from the boneyard. If you run out of space, start turning corners with the pieces. The first player to use up all his or her pebbles wins!

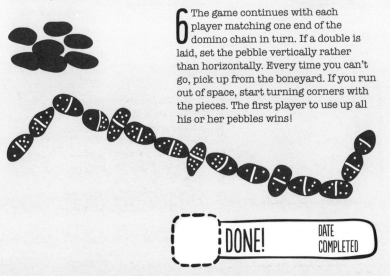

DONE!

DATE COMPLETED

62 PLAY WATER BALLOON DODGE

Cool off on a hot day, and invite your friends to a friendly water balloon fight. But be prepared to get wet—VERY wet!

1 Get your ammunition ready. Before filling up each balloon with water, blow it up and stretch it a little. This should stop it from popping. Stretch the neck of the balloon over the end of a tap or hose. Turn on a medium stream of water so that it doesn't shoot off! Turn the water off before the balloon is filled to the top.

2 Tie the balloons tightly, a few inches from the top. Put them in buckets. This can take a while, so ask your friends to help!

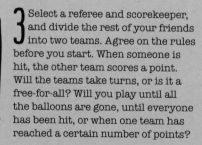

3 Select a referee and scorekeeper, and divide the rest of your friends into two teams. Agree on the rules before you start. When someone is hit, the other team scores a point. Will the teams take turns, or is it a free-for-all? Will you play until all the balloons are gone, until everyone has been hit, or when one team has reached a certain number of points?

DONE! DATE COMPLETED

GO HILL ROLLING 63

Want an exciting activity that is faster and more fun than walking? Try Mother Nature's very own roller coaster—go hill rolling!

1 Find a grassy hill. It needs to have a good slope, but make sure that it's not too steep. Make sure there are no rocks, litter, or animal droppings!

2 Empty your pockets and hand everything over to a friend. (It's pretty uncomfortable rolling over and over your things, plus you might lose something!)

3 Lay down on the ground at the top of the hill. Either cross your arms in front of you or put your arms above you.

4 And . . . roll! If there are other rollers, shout out "Wheeee!" so they know you're coming. Did you have fun? OK, so walk to the other side of the hill, get up to the top, and roll again and again!

SAFETY FIRST!
To be super safe, wear a helmet and knee pads.

DONE! | DATE COMPLETED

64 BUILD A WOODLAND DEN

If you go down to the woods today, why not build yourself a den? You don't need to take anything with you—all the materials will be in the woodland itself. A couple of friends would be a great help, though!

1 Find some open woodland to build your den. Look for a place with flat ground. Find two strong branches with forked ends for uprights. Drive them into the ground, a couple of yards apart, making sure they're at the same height.

2 Now you need to find a strong branch to sit across the forked uprights. This will be your ridge pole. Make sure that your structure is sturdy. If not, drive your uprights into the ground a little more.

3 Gather up lots of strong, long sticks from the woodland floor. Only use dead wood—don't break any branches from the trees. Lean the sticks up against your ridge pole. Place them evenly on both sides. It's best to put a few on one side, then a few on the other, and so on, so that one side doesn't get too heavy and fall down.

4 Continue to add sticks and branches until you have made a tent-shaped structure. Use as many sticks as possible to fill in the gaps. You can either close off one end in the same way, or leave both ends open.

5 Now you're going to thatch. Collect leaves from the forest floor, and pile them up against your structure. Start from the bottom, and work your way up. You can also use moss, pine needles, or bracken—anything you can find that is dead. Don't pull branches or leaves from the trees.

6 When you've finished thatching, go inside! It should be snug and warm in your woodland den—a perfect place to while away the hours with good friends.

DONE! DATE COMPLETED

65 CATCH THE DRAGON TAIL

This is a traditional Chinese game inspired by the legendary Chinese dragon of ancient mythology. It's best played in a large group—perfect for a party! You need at least 10 people, but the more the merrier!

1 Choose a referee. Everyone else should make at least 3 teams. If possible, each team should have the same number of members. Line up the teams to face each other.

2 Tie or loop a scarf to the back of the last person in the line of each team. These are the dragon's tails. The people at the front of the lines are the dragons' heads. Everyone should hold onto the waist or shoulders of the person in front of them.

3 When the referee shouts "Catch the dragon tail," the game begins. The dragon heads need to get the scarves, or tails, from the other teams. The team lines must not break, and no one but the dragon heads are allowed to catch the tails.

4 When a tail is caught, the head shouts "caught" and the referee awards the team a point. If a line is broken or anyone but the heads catches the tail, the team loses a point. The referee needs to write down the scores.

5 The scarf is given back to the "tail," and the game continues. You can either play for a set amount of time or until one team has reached 5 points. The team with the most points is the winner!

DONE! DATE COMPLETED

66 MAKE A GEYSER

If you like messy, dramatic experiments, this is one for you! With just a bottle of diet cola and a packet of Mentos sweets, you can create a mighty geyser. Some people say theirs have been 29 feet tall! How high can you make yours?

1 Find an open space where you can make a mess. Go as far away as possible from anyone's nice clean windows or anything else you don't want to get sticky and yucky!

2 Stand the bottle of cola upright and unscrew the lid. If you have a funnel, put it into the top of the bottle.

3 Drop about half a packet of Mentos into the bottle through the funnel, and get out of the way! Stand far back to watch a mighty, bubbly geyser erupt from the bottle!

DONE!
DATE COMPLETED

GO ON A NATURE HUNT

67

Get together with a couple of friends and challenge them to a nature hunt. Decide as a group what to look for and what to do with your treasures at the end.

IDEAS LIST

Things that are:
Round, fuzzy, green, hard, soft, beautiful, red, orange, light, heavy

Something you can: Fly, spin, twirl, make a noise with

Make something from:
A pinecone, 3 different leaves, 5 seeds, a flower, a berry, a feather

1 Make sure that each hunter has a grocery bag, a pen, and some paper. Sit and agree on a list of things to look for. As you agree on an item to hunt, write it down. You'll each need a copy of the list.

2 Agree on where you'll go—perhaps in your back garden or in the park. Make sure that an adult always knows where you are.

3 Find every item on the list and put it in your bag. Do not pick flowers or leaves— try to find them on the ground.

4 When you've finished, make sure that everyone else has too. Take your stuff home to compare—you can make a little exhibition with the best finds.

DONE! DATE COMPLETED

68 SKETCH A TREE

Do you have a favorite tree in your garden or on your way to school? Why not capture it on paper? It's easy if you focus on one part at a time.

YOU WILL NEED:

- Paper
- Pencil
- Pencil sharpener
- Erase
- Cushion to sit on (optional)

1 Sit down in front of your favorite tree, and get comfy. Look carefully at its overall shape, trunk, branches, and leaves. You're going to start drawing it from the bottom and work your way up. Draw the sides of the tree trunk and any roots at the base of the tree.

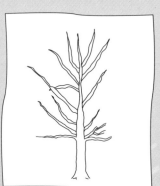

2 Now draw the main branches. Notice how they get thinner as they spread out. Allow some branches to be behind others. Include the unusual shapes that branches often make.

3 Draw the bark patterns on the trunk and branches. Add as much detail as possible. Shadows and lines will make it more realistic.

4 Draw the smaller branches and twigs. Notice how the smaller twigs branch off the larger ones, and even smaller twigs branch off of those.

5 Now add some softer marks for the leaves. You don't need to draw every leaf on its own.

6 Take a look at where the shadow falls on your tree. Start with the trunk, and add shade and tone. Now shade the branches that fall into shadow. Shade the leaves last. When you've finished, don't forget to sign your masterpiece!

DONE!   DATE COMPLETED

69 TOAST MARSHMALLOWS

Whether you're sitting around a fire on the beach at night, snuggling around a campfire in the woods, or just having a barbecue, it's the perfect time to toast some marshmallows—YUMMY!

1 Poke a marshmallow onto a stick. Make sure that the end of the stick goes through the other end of the marshmallow so that it won't slip off into the fire.

2 Put the marshmallow over (not in) the fire or hot barbecue coals. Rotate the stick to cook it evenly. If you like your marshmallow gooey, take it away from the fire as soon as it's puffed up, or wait until it turns a golden brown color on the outside.

3 Remove the marshmallow from the fire. Let it cool for a minute. Then bite off the marshmallow from its stick and let it melt in your mouth. Delicious! Time for another?

WHY NOT?
Add toppings? Dip your toasted marshmallows into chocolate or caramel sauce, and then cover in chopped nuts!

SAFETY FIRST
Never light a fire without an adult. If your marshmallow catches fire, blow it out, don't shake it.

DONE!

DATE COMPLETED

USE NATURAL DYES

Try out nature's very own dyes. Experiment with different leaves, berries, and vegetables to see which colors you can make and which work best.

YOU WILL NEED:

- Salt
- Light-colored old T-shirt or scarf
- An old saucepan
- Knife
- Spoon
- Plants, fruits, or vegetables (like blueberries, carrots, and beetroot)
- Rubber gloves
- Sieve

1 Pick the vegetables or berries that you want to use. Ask an adult to help you chop them up. Put them in an old saucepan, and then half fill it with water. Ask an adult to bring it to the boil, simmer for about an hour, and strain.

2 Adding salt and cold water will help the dye stay on the fabric. Add half a cup of salt to every 8 cups of water. Soak your T-shirt in the fixative (the salt and water) for about an hour. Rinse your T-shirt in cool water until it runs clear.

3 Wearing gloves, put your T-shirt into the dye. Press it down until it's completely covered. Leave overnight. Wearing gloves, remove it from the pan, wring it out, and hang it up to dry.

DONE!   DATE COMPLETED

71 BUILD A SNOW PENGUIN

I bet you've built a snowman, but how about a
snow penguin? It can look very cute in all that
amazing snowfall and is actually based on the
traditional snowman shape.

1 Wrap up warm, and don't forget
your gloves! (In fact, take a
spare pair or two for when they
get wet.) First, make the base. Roll
a large ball of snow, just as you
would for building a snowman.
Leave where you want your
penguin, with the flattest side up.

2 Roll another ball of snow that is
about two-thirds the size of the
first ball. Put it on top of your
base. Now make one more ball of
snow that is about half the size
of the second one. It should be as
round as possible. Put it on top.

3 Fill the gaps between the
snowballs with more snow.
Smooth and pat the snow
down. Keep adding more snow
and smoothing it down until you
have a pear-shaped "body."

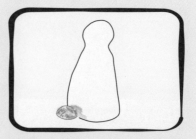

4 Gather snow around the base,
and shape it into two feet. Use
your fingers or a stick to make
gaps between the "claws" so the feet
look webbed.

5 Now add the penguin's wings. Draw a wing shape on each side with your finger. Carve out the shape so the groove is clear, and then add snow. Pat and shape the snow to fill out the wings.

6 The beak is the most delicate bit, so don't worry if it takes a few tries. It's easiest to have a stick support to build around. Find a stick that's a little longer than the length you'd like for your beak, and stick it into your penguin's head. Pack snow around the beak and shape it into a beak shape as you go.

7 And lastly, the tail! Gather up snow to form a tail shape directly from the penguin's base on the snow. Now the body is finished! If you spray your penguin lightly with water from a spray bottle or hose, it will freeze solid and last longer.

8 Now add eyes with small stones and maybe a hat and a scarf for fun! Don't forget to take a photo!

DONE!

DATE COMPLETED

72 SPIN A PICTURE

Watch out for flying paint! You should wear old clothes that you don't mind getting dirty for this project. If you don't know Damien Hirst's spin paintings, look them up on the Internet, and see if yours match up.

YOU WILL NEED:

- Paper plate
- Adhesive tape
- Small amount of modeling clay
- Thumbtack
- Poster paint
- Shallow box (big enough for the plate to sit inside with space around the sides)
- Thick paintbrush

1 Stick some tape onto the back of the plate, in the middle. Push the thumbtack through the center of the other side of the plate, through the tape.

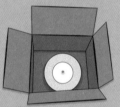

2 Put the modeling clay into the middle of the bottom of the box. Push the plate onto the clay blob with the thumbtack. Try spinning the plate. Adjust it up or down to spin as smoothly as possible.

3 Take some paint onto your brush and drip it onto the plate, spinning the plate at the same time. Add as many colors as you like, but keep spinning! When you have a spin picture that you like, let it dry. Then make enough to make a spin picture gallery.

TOP TIP

If you have a salad spinner, you could use that! Just put your plate inside, drip on the paint, and spin!

DONE!   DATE COMPLETED

PLAY RED LIGHT, GREEN LIGHT

Can you react quickly and stay as still as a statue? Grab some friends, find a big playing area, and give it a try!

1 Decide who is going to be the "traffic light." He or she stands at one end of the playing field. All of the other players stand behind a line at the other end of the playing field facing the "light."

2 The "light" turns away from the other players. When he or she says GREEN LIGHT, the players run toward the "light." When the "light" says RED LIGHT, he or she turns around and the players must freeze.

3 If players wobble or fall, they are sent back to the starting line.

4 The goal is to tag the "light" on the shoulder and become the "light" yourself. The "light" needs to try to trick the other players into wobbling or falling by turning around suddenly and quickly.

DONE! DATE COMPLETED

[74] MAKE RANGOLI PATTERNS

Swirling bright colors in intricate patterns are laid on doorsteps and courtyards in India during the festival of lights—Dewali. They are called rangoli, and they welcome guests into people's homes.

YOU WILL NEED:

- Table salt (the more you have, the bigger your design)
- Runny paints (craft/poster/ tempura paint) in 3 different colors (you can use whatever 3 colors you like)
- Bowl
- Spoon
- Doorstep, paved area, patio, or driveway outside your home

1 Pour one-third of your table salt into a bowl. Add a spoonful of one of your runny paints and stir until it has mixed into the salt evenly. Add more paint if you want a stronger color. Make the other two colors with the rest of the salt, then leave to dry out overnight.

2 Find a place to display your rangoli. It is traditional to put it near the entrance to your home, so maybe on your driveway, pavement, patio, or courtyard. Make sure that it won't get in anyone's way. Sweep the area first so you have a clean surface.

3 Take a handful of the first colored salt, and place it in the center of your chosen space. Shape it into a circle.

4 Take a little of the next colored salt in the palm of your hand. Use your thumb and forefinger to sprinkle it neatly around the edge of your circle. Neaten it with the tips of your fingers.

5 Take a handful of the last colored salt, and place it above the circle. Add another 6 handfuls, and round them off to become petals.

6 Use the rest of your first colored salt to create a frame around the petals.

7 Add handfuls of salt to the dips in the flower's frame, and shape to finish off. You can add nightlights around your rangoli pattern to make it especially welcoming. When you want to make a different design, simply sweep the salt away and start all over again!

DONE! DATE COMPLETED

75 SPRAY-PAINT STATIONERY

Personalize your stationery with spray paint and found objects. You can create all sorts of patterns and textures for that special thank-you note, birthday card, or wrapping paper.

YOU WILL NEED:

- Empty spray bottles
- Paint
- Water
- Thick paper or blank writing paper
- Newspaper
- Found objects (leaves, pebbles, shells, feathers, recycled materials)

1 Wash the spray bottles out thoroughly. Squeeze the colored paints into different bottles and add water. They shouldn't be too runny. Spray some onto some old newspaper to check the consistency.

2 Lay the newspaper on the lawn or patio, and put your blank paper on top. Arrange collected objects such as pebbles, leaves, feathers, or other interestingly shaped recycled materials onto the paper.

3 Spray the paint mixture over the paper and objects. Leave to dry, and then remove the objects carefully to reveal your spray-paint patterns.

DONE! DATE COMPLETED

TAKE YOUR CAMERA FOR A WALK

When you walk to school or go shopping, do you really notice everything that's around you? If you take your camera for a walk, you might just start to see everything in a brand-new light.

1 Decide on a walk. It might be a routine journey to school or the walk to a friend's house. It could be somewhere new, for example, when you're on vacation. Always let an adult know where you're going.

2 As you walk, keep your eyes peeled for great photo opportunities. What catches your eye? Is there something you always look out for? Do you meet the neighborhood cat? Is there anything funny?

3 It's always exciting to look at the pictures you've taken. You could print them out, order, and write on them or make a slide show on your computer. Share them with your friends and family, and ask them to guess where they were taken.

DONE!

DATE COMPLETED

77 MAKE YOUR OWN HAMMOCK

Have a lazy outdoor day, gently swinging in a hammock. If you don't already have one, make your own! All you need is a sheet, some climbing rope, and an adult to hang it up for you.

YOU WILL NEED:

- 1 large bed sheet (not too old and worn)
- 2×2 ft utility cord (available from climbing shops and hardware stores)
- 2×3 ft webbing (available from climbing shops and hardware stores)
- Adult help

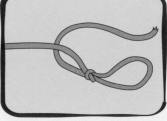

1 Take one piece of cord and make a loop at the end. Secure with a double knot. Leave a 4-inch (10 cm) "tail."

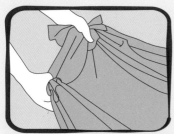

2 Loosely zigzag fold, or gather your sheet lengthwise. Then fold over one of the width ends at about 8 inches.

3 Gather the fabric from both sides about 4 inches in from the edge. Hold with your fist.

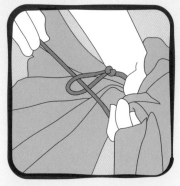

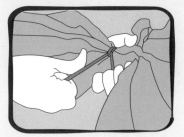

4 Wrap the cord around the sheet where your fist is, and then thread the cord through the loop.

5 Pull the cord until the loop is tight to the sheet. Wrap the cord tightly around the sheet 5 or 6 times, and tie the two ends together with a secure double knot.

6 Thread one piece of webbing through the end of your sheet. Tie a secure knot in your webbing. Repeat these steps on the other side.

7 Your hammock is now ready for an adult to hang up for you. Ask him or her to check that your knots are secure first, and to tighten them if necessary.

SAFETY FIRST

An adult needs to check that your knots are tight enough and hang your hammock up for you. Strong trees, beams, and branches are all great places to hang your hammock. Be sure not to hang it too high up.

DONE! DATE COMPLETED

78 RACE MINI JUNK RAFTS

Get creative with recycled trash, and build the ultimate mini raft. Get your friends to make one too, and race them in the park on a breezy day.

YOU WILL NEED:

- String or rubber bands
- Recycled and found bits and pieces—plastic trays and bottles, straws, corks, bamboo, craft sticks, bottle tops, twigs, pinecones, feathers, etc.
- Inventive and competitive friends!

1 Gather lots of useful stuff. Think about whether they will float. Cardboard will soak and sink, but an old flat cheese grater might stay above the water if fixed to a couple of plastic bottles. Combine man-made and natural materials. Be inventive, and think outside the box!

2 Decide on your raft's shape. It doesn't have to be square. Lay the materials out and arrange them. Fix the pieces together with string or rubber bands, or both.

3 Name your raft and challenge your friends to a race. A breezy day on a shallow pond in the local park is perfect. But make sure that it is safe to wade in afterward to retrieve your inventions!

 DONE!　　DATE COMPLETED

TRY STONE SKIMMING

When you visit the seaside, a lake, or a river, try to beat the stone skimming record of 51 bounces. It takes practice, but if at first you don't succeed, try, try again!

1 Find a flat stretch of water with a good supply of rocks. Look for a skinny, flat, oval rock about the size of your palm.

2 Hold the stone between your thumb and forefinger in your strongest hand. Imagine the rock's path, choosing a spot ahead of you where you want the first bounce to be. Angle your hand so the front of the stone is pointing slightly upward.

3 Keep your elbow close to your body and swing out from your hip. Swing your arm in an arc. As your arm reaches the bottom of the arc, straighten it and flick your wrist to release the stone.

TOP TIP
The smoother and flatter the stone, the better it will skip across the surface of the water without breaking the surface tension.

DONE!   DATE COMPLETED

80 PRESS FLOWERS

Keep summer alive forever! Pressed flowers are perfect for framing, decorating, or even placing inside a locket. There are lots of ways to press them, but here is the simplest way.

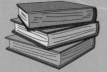

1 Find a heavy book. Encyclopedias or dictionaries are ideal. The moisture from the flowers might wrinkle the pages, so make sure the book isn't precious to someone!

2 Lay the book open somewhere near the middle. Line it with two sheets of paper on either side. Cut the paper to fit if you need to. The outer two sheets are your "blotters."

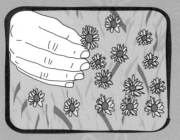

3 For best results, pick your flowers when they're at the height of their bloom, when their color is at its brightest. Choose flowers with fresh petals that haven't started to droop or die and that aren't damaged by insects.

4 Ideally, pick flowers when they are dry. But if you pick flowers that are still wet with dew or rain, allow them to dry completely before you press them. Dab them gently with a paper towel to speed the drying process.

5 Lay your flowers on one side of the book. Arrange them with spaces in between, and not too close to the paper edge. Do not overlap, unless you want your finished pressed flowers to do so.

6 To press flowers with a conical shape (like tulips or roses), cut them in half lengthwise, or press individual petals.

7 If you have a lot of flowers, line other pages of your book with four sheets of paper, and use those too. But make sure that you leave about half an inch between the different pages that you're using to press the flowers.

8 Close the book very carefully, without disturbing your flower arrangement or the paper alignment. Pile more heavy books on top of the pressing book. Leave in a dry place in your home.

9 Change the paper sheets every few days. Do this very carefully so you don't disturb the delicate flowers. After a couple of weeks, the flowers will be completely dry. Remove carefully with your fingers or a pair of tweezers.

DONE! DATE COMPLETED

81 MAKE A COLANDER WIND CHIME

You can't beat the soft jingle of a wind chime blowing in the breeze. You can use all sorts of bits and pieces to make one. Use your imagination!

YOU WILL NEED:

- Fishing line (ideally) or string
- An old colander (or any other plastic or metal object with holes, for example, a cheese grater)
- Bits and pieces that you can thread or tie, such as beads, keys, shells, buttons, pinecones, paper clips—whatever you like!

1 Measure and cut six pieces of fishing line, about 30 inches long. Gather together all of your found bits and pieces.

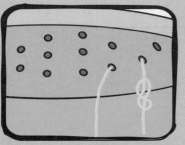

2 Thread one piece of fishing line through two holes just above the circular rim of your colander. Pull through until you have half the length hanging from each hole. Tie knots in the middle of the fishing line to fix it securely. The two threads should dangle down.

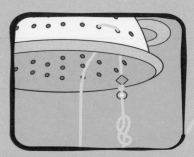

3 Thread or tie your treasures onto each side of the fishing line, one at a time. Each time you slide a bead or button onto the string, tie a knot beneath it. Make sure that the knot is big enough to stop them from sliding down.

4 It is best to leave your very dangly bits, such as keys, for the bottom of the line. Just tie them on, and knot in place.

5 Put one piece of line to the side. Thread and decorate the rest as in steps 2 to 4. Space them out evenly around the colander.

6 Take the last piece of fishing line and tie each end to the handles of the colander. This is for hanging it up. Now just wait for a soft breeze to work its magic.

WHY NOT?
Ask an adult to help you to hang your wind chime outside near your bedroom window.

DONE!

DATE COMPLETED

82 MAKE ANGELS IN THE SNOW

Here's how to make perfect angels in the snow. If you go out right after a snowfall, you'll have a blank canvas to work on.

1 Find a patch of snow that's at least as tall as your body and as wide as your outstretched arms. Fresh powdery snow is best, so if possible, do this immediately after snowfall. Carefully fall back onto the snow with your arms outstretched.

2 Move your arms and legs back and forth, keeping them straight as if you're doing a jumping jack. Press your head back hard enough to make sure that you're leaving a good imprint.

3 Get up carefully so you don't spoil your masterpiece. If a friend is with you, ask him or her to help you up. Stand back and admire your snow angel. Take a photo!

DONE!   DATE COMPLETED

WIN AN EGG AND SPOON RACE

Have you ever been in an egg and spoon race?
Gather a few friends to race against, or compete
against the clock to become an egg-spert!

1 Cook the eggs in boiling water for about 8 minutes so that they're hard. Let them cool down before you use them. Its best to have a grown-up around for this step!

YOU WILL NEED:

- Enough eggs for each of your competitors
- Spoons to balance the eggs on
- Sticks and/or ropes
- An adult to help you

2 Decide on your racecourse, and mark the start and finish lines with ropes or sticks. Pick out a spoon that's big enough to fit your egg on it but not so big that the egg rolls around.

3 Hold one arm out in front of you with the egg and spoon almost at eye height. Keep your head and arm as still as you possibly can while running as smoothly as you can. Avoid any sudden movements! Keep your eye on the finish line, and try not to drop your egg. If you drop your egg, you must go back to the beginning!

DONE!   DATE COMPLETED

[84] BUILD A SPUDZOOKA

Air pressure can be extremely powerful. It's even been used to launch satellites into space! This potato cannon (or spudzooka) uses the power of pressure to send potato pieces a long way!

YOU WILL NEED:

- A length of copper piping, 12-24 inches
- Dowel or garden cane
- Large raw potato
- Metal nail file
- An adult to help you

SAFETY FIRST!

Never fire your spudzooka at people or animals. Do this with an adult. You must always be outdoors in a large space.

1 Find a length of copper piping. If you don't have any, ask for an offcut at your local hardware store. They may cut it to size for you, too. Otherwise, ask an adult to cut it to between 12 and 24 inches long.

2 Make sure that the pipe is straight and that the ends are smooth. If there are any rough edges, ask an adult to file them down for you. Do not touch the ends before they are filed down, as they may cut you.

3 Time to "load" your spudzooka. Put the potato onto a table (make sure you protect the table first) and hold it with one hand. With the other hand, push one end of the pipe all the way through the potato.

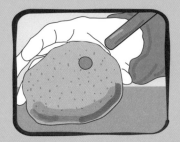

4 Push the other end of the pipe through the potato in the same way as before. Take the pipe out. Now you should have potato in both ends of the piping.

5 Line the pipe up and aim at a target. Poke one end of your spudzooka with the dowel and keep poking until it "fires."

6 To use your spudzooka again, push out the potato that's still there with your dowel, and reload, as in steps 3 and 4.

WHY NOT?
Make a target for your spudzooka. Dip the end of the potato in paint so you can see where it hits. Bull's-eye!

DONE! DATE COMPLETED

85 CREATE YOUR OWN WALK OF FAME

Since the 1920s, famous movie stars have left their handprints in paving stones on Hollywood Boulevard. It's part of the Walk of Fame. Why not recreate it in your own backyard, but this time, you and your family are the stars?

YOU WILL NEED:

- A disposable container (for example, plastic plant dish or even a sturdy cardboard box will do)
- Disposable plastic gloves
- Bucket
- Powdered cement mix
- Vegetable oil and brush
- Trowel or putty knife
- Stick or pencil
- Small toys, trinkets, or glass pebbles

1 Put on your gloves, and then mix the powdered cement and water in the bucket according to the instructions on the packaging. It should become a thick paste.

2 Brush a little bit of vegetable oil into the base of your container. Pour in the cement and smooth the top with the trowel. Let it sit for about an hour.

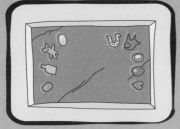

3 Leave a space that will be large enough for your handprints. Decorate the rest with your trinkets and pebbles. Try to use objects that say something about you. For example, an old but special toy car or something that is your favorite color.

4 Use the stick to write your name or initials. You could also add the date. Remove your gloves, spread out your fingers and press firmly to make a print in the cement. Wash your hands thoroughly immediately after.

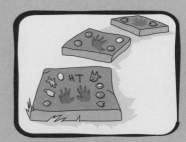

5 Let the stone sit for a few days before getting it out of its container.

6 When you've made a stone with each member of the family, lay them out on your lawn or backyard, and celebrate with an opening ceremony!

SAFETY FIRST!

Wash your hands thoroughly with soap and water as soon as you've made your handprints in the cement.

DONE!

DATE COMPLETED

86 BUILD A BUG HOTEL

Bugs are great for the garden, and they're fascinating too. Make a "hotel" for them to shelter in during the cold winter months, and see who checks in. But be patient! It might take several months before your visitors decide to stay.

1 Get some large, plastic soda bottles and remove any labels. Ask an adult to help you to cut off the bottoms with a pair of sharp scissors. Keep the tops screwed on.

2 Line each bottle with corrugated card. This will make it dark inside the bottle.

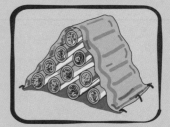

3 Fill each bottle with nesting materials like straw, dry leaves, small twigs, moss, and bark. Pack them in as tightly as possible so they don't fall out.

4 Stack the bottles into a pyramid shape, and cover them with felting or plastic. Weigh the "roof" down with logs or tent pegs so that it doesn't blow away. Check your hotel regularly to make sure that it's intact as well as to spot the visitors!

DONE! DATE COMPLETED

GO ROCK POOLING

Rock pools are great little open-air aquariums. When you're at the seaside, pick up a bucket and take a look!

1 Before you set out, get a bucket and a net, and make sure that you've checked the tide times carefully. Stay away from any cliffs. Put a little seawater into your bucket, and start hunting!

2 Think like a marine creature—they like shady, protected spots, so look under rocks, among seaweed, and between cracks in the rocks. Carefully dig with your fingers to see what you can find.

3 Pick up creatures carefully and put them in your bucket or container for a closer look. Some may be very small or camouflaged against the sand or weeds. Always put creatures back where you found them, and make sure that you return them the right way up.

SAFETY FIRST

Check the tides on the Internet or at your local tourist office before you go. The best time to go is during the very low tides. Head out an hour or two before low tide to give yourself plenty of time to get back safely. Be careful of the slippery rocks near the shore.

DONE!   DATE COMPLETED

88 MAKE AND PLAY LADYBUG TIC-TAC-TOE

You might know this game as naughts and crosses. The ancient Romans called it Terni Lapilli. Whatever you call it, it's super cool when you have pet ladybug rocks to play with!

YOU WILL NEED:

- 10 smooth flat stones
- Acrylic paints in red, black, white, blue, and yellow
- Chalk
- Paintbrushes
- Sticks and twigs
- Garden string

1 Find 10 ladybug-shaped stones in your garden or park. Paint 5 of them red and the other 5 yellow. Give them a couple of coats of paint to make sure they're well covered. Let them dry thoroughly between coats.

2 Use chalk to mark the head and wing line on each. Use a thinner brush to paint over the wing line with black paint, then paint in the head. You can rub off the chalk when it's dry.

3 Now add the dots. You can either paint on the dots with a brush or dip a finger into the paint and finger paint them on.

4 When the black paint is dry, add other details—eyes, mouth, nose, and antenna. The end of the paintbrush is great for making dots for the antenna.

5 When you've painted all 10 stones, you have all the pieces for the game. Make the grid by crisscrossing sticks and branches on the ground. You can make them sturdy by tying them with string.

6 Play tic-tac-toe! One player uses the red ladybugs, the other uses the yellow ladybugs. Take it in turns to place a ladybug in a square. The first to get 3 in a row wins!

DONE!

DATE
COMPLETED

89 GROW MINT TEA

Mint tea is refreshing, delicious, and good for you!
A pot of freshly grown mint makes your house or
garden smell wonderful too.

YOU WILL NEED:

To grow your mint:
- Small pot (12 inches is ideal)
- Compost
- Small mint plant (you can buy
  many different varieties)
- Small stones or gravel
- Sunny window ledge, patio, or
  doorstep

To make your tea:
- A bunch of mint leaves
- Sugar or honey to taste
- Boiling water (ask an adult
  to do this for you)
- Mug or a heatproof glass

1 If you can, plant your mint in spring, or in the fall if you're in a climate that is free of frost. Plant your mint 2 inches deep in a 12-inch pot.

2 Put your pot in a sunny position. Ideally, it will receive morning sunlight and have some shade in the afternoon. Keep it well watered so that the soil is always damp.

3 Keep the top of your plant well trimmed to stop it from growing too tall. This will encourage growth at the sides.

4 For your mint tea, pinch a stem or two of mint from your plant, and rinse under cold water. Crush the leaves a bit as you put them into the bottom of your mug to help bring out the minty taste and smell.

5 Ask an adult to boil a kettle and pour the boiling water over your leaves. Leave it to cool down a little before you try it!

6 Add sugar or honey to taste. You can even add a squeeze of citrus (lemon or lime) if you want to add a tasty zing!

WHY NOT?
Add to new potatoes or carrots? Mint can be used for all sorts of cooking. You can add it to cold drinks such as lemonade too.

DONE! DATE COMPLETED

90 GET WET IN THE WATER RELAY!

This is a fun game to play with a couple of friends on a hot day. You'll need a plastic drinking cup and a bucket each as well as a giant bucket of water. And yes—the water is supposed to drip down your nose!

1 Ask an adult to poke 6 holes into the sides of each cup using a thick sewing needle. Make sure there are the same number of holes in each player's cup!

2 Choose a grassy area with a lot of space. Put the empty buckets in a line on the ground a little apart from one another. Put the giant bucket full of water at the other end of that area.

3 Players start at the big bucket of water. When someone shouts GO, they fill their cups with water at the same time. The players hold their cups above their heads and run to their empty buckets.

4 As the players reach their buckets, they should tip any water left in their cup into it and race back to the other end. The first to fill his or her bucket right up to the top wins! On your marks, get set . . . GO!

DONE!   DATE COMPLETED

WORK OUT THE AGE OF A TREE

91

If a tree has been cut down, you can work out how old it was when it died by counting its rings. But if the tree is alive, there's another way to calculate its age.

1 Decide on the tree that you want to find the age of. Wrap your tape measure around the trunk, and measure its circumference, or girth.

40IN
——
1
= 40 YEARS OLD

2 If you've measured in inches, divide by 1. If you have measured in centimeters, divide this figure by 2.5. The growth of an average tree girth per year is 1 inch, or 2.5 centimeters. So a tree with a 16-inch (40-cm) girth will be approximately 16 years old.

3 If you know the species of your tree, you can age it more accurately. For example, oaks and beeches grow approximately 0.7 inches per year. Pine trees grow about 1.2 inches per year, and sycamores grow around 1.1 inches per year. Divide by these figures instead of 1 inch.

BEECH

SYCAMORE

PINE

OAK

DONE!   DATE COMPLETED

92 HANG A WREATH

Welcome visitors to your door by hanging a wreath! Use leaves and stems collected from your garden or local area at any time of the year. Berries and flowers add a great splash of color.

YOU WILL NEED:

- Florist foam ring with a plastic bottom
- Ribbon
- Scissors
- Foliage, for example, sprigs of fir, holly, ivy, mistletoe, rosemary, lavender, flowers, berries— anything that you can find with a stem!

1 Collect foliage. Sprigs of fir, holly, and berried ivy all work well. But anything with a stem will work! Use scissors to cut stems about 10 cm long. Ask permission before you pick anything!

2 Remove 1 inch of leaves or needles from each sprig so that you have stems to press into the foam. Either trim with scissors or remove them with your fingers.

3 Float the foam ring facedown into a bowl or sink of water and allow it to sink naturally. Do not force it under. After about a minute it will turn dark green. Take it out.

4 Insert sprigs of one plant into your foam at regular intervals. Angle the sprigs to follow the shape of the wreath.

5 Insert leaves or sprigs of different plants at different angles, still following the wreath's outline. Make sure you cover all parts of the foam equally. Keep going until you have filled all the gaps in the wreath.

6 Thread the ribbon through the center of the wreath. Tie a knot at the top so that you can hang it. If you want to, tie a bow instead of a knot. Hang on your door to welcome all your visitors!

DONE!   DATE COMPLETED

93 PING A MASTERPIECE

This is fun, messy art, perfect for doing outdoors. You'll ping a masterpiece together in no time!

YOU WILL NEED:

- Rubber bands (different thicknesses if possible)
- Sponge
- Different colored paints
- Paintbrush
- Cardboard (for example, the side of a cereal box)
- White paper that is twice as wide as the cardboard
- Containers for paint mixing

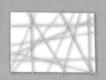

1 Fold the white paper around the cardboard to cover both sides. Stretch and wrap the rubber bands over it to make a pattern of lines.

2 Squeeze colored paints into different containers. Dip sponges into the paints and dab them onto the paper with the rubber bands. For clean colors, use a different sponge for each paint.

3 Use the paintbrush to drip some paint onto a couple of the bands and ping them. The colors will splash over the paper randomly.

4 Let your art dry on one side, and then paint the other. When the second side is dry, remove the rubber bands and unfold the paper to see the patterns you've created.

WHY NOT?
Use your rubber band art as wrapping paper or stationery?

DONE!   DATE COMPLETED

GO POND DIPPING 94

Discover a hidden world in a pond. You'll need a net, a shallow tray, a magnifying glass, rain boots, and a pond field guide.

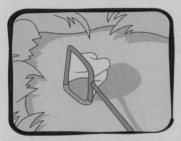

1 First, fill your tray with pond water. Then gently sweep your net around the pond through the vegetation. Creatures live on the top, the middle, and the bottom of the pond, so make sure you sweep in all areas. You want to disturb some of the sediment at the bottom.

2 Turn your net inside out over your tray so that any creatures and plants fall out. What can you see? Don't forget to look under and on the vegetation. Creatures will hide in your tray just as they do in the pond. Can you identify any of them in your field guide?

3 For a closer look, scoop up a creature and some water into a smaller pot with a lid. Use your magnifying glass and check your field guide to see what you've found!

SAFETY FIRST!

Always go pond dipping with an adult. Stand at the edge of the pond rather than wading in, and don't lean over too far. Always put the creatures back where you found them when you're done.

DONE! DATE COMPLETED

95 LAUNCH A VINEGAR ROCKET

Baking soda and vinegar make brilliant rocket fuel! Try mixing them together in an empty drink bottle to launch your very own rocket.

YOU WILL NEED:

- 1 empty plastic bottle
- 1 piece of white tissue
- 1 cork
- 3 pencils
- Adhesive tape
- Baking soda
- Vinegar
- Safety goggles

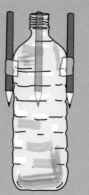

1 Tape the pencils to the side of the bottle in a triangle to make fins. The bottom ends of the pencils should be facing upward. The ends should line up at the bottle top.

2 Make the baking soda parcel. Put two large spoonfuls of baking soda into the middle of the tissue. Fold the corners up and twist the wrap to hold the powder inside.

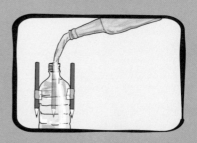

3 Fill the bottle about a third of the way up with vinegar. Any vinegar works, but white vinegar is less messy.

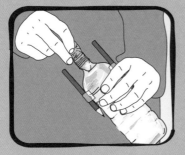

4 Make sure you are outside before you do this step. Carefully push the baking soda parcel into the top of the bottle. Ask an adult to help you to push the cork firmly into the bottle top.

5 Gently shake the bottle, making sure you keep it away from your face. Quickly stand the rocket up on its fins and move away.

6 Stand well back and wait for LIFT-OFF!

HOW DOES IT WORK?

When the baking soda and vinegar react, carbon dioxide is released, creating pressure in the bottle. When the pressure gets high enough, it will push the cork out and the pressure will force all of the liquid and gas out of the bottle very fast, making it shoot upward.

SAFETY FIRST!

Always do this with an adult. Stay well away from the bottle. You MUST be outdoors in a large space.

DONE! DATE COMPLETED

96 MAKE A BIRD BATH

Birds might fly several miles to find clean drinking water. Why not tempt them into your garden or onto your balcony with a bird bath?

YOU WILL NEED:

- Plant pot or bucket
- Saucer (ideally with a rough surface)
- Garden paint
- Waterproof glue or tile adhesive
- Pebbles
- Water

1 Find an old plant pot or bucket. Turn it upside down and paint it. Be imaginative with colors, patterns, and pictures.

2 Now paint the saucer. Ideally use one with a rough surface for the birds' feet to grip without slipping. Terra-cotta plant saucers are perfect. Leave the pot and saucer to dry overnight.

3 Glue around the top of the upturned pot. Place the saucer on top, making sure that it is positioned in the middle. Press firmly, and allow the glue to set.

4 Find a safe place to put your birdbath. Nearby branches are useful for birds to hop to safety from a swooping bird of prey or a hungry cat!

5 Pile up some pebbles on one side of the saucer. The birds can perch on these. They will also provide a spot for insects to lie in the sun.

6 Fill the saucer with water, making sure that the pebbles are slightly above the waterline to make a perch. Perfect! The birds now have a spot to drink.

WHY NOT?

Set up a wildlife camera to record your visitors? You can note which birds come to visit during different times of the year!

DONE!

DATE COMPLETED

97 CREATE A BOOT GARDEN

Don't get rid of your old rain boots—use them to create an awesome garden! If you want to get really carried away, find more boots and shoes in your local thrift store.

1 Find some old rain boots. If there aren't holes in them already, ask an adult to make some holes in the bottom to allow for drainage (using a hand drill and large drill bit).

2 Pour sand or grit into the bottom of each foot to add weight and stop them from falling over. It will also help with drainage. Fill them to the top with potting soil or compost.

3 Plant them with seeds, bulbs or potting plants, and arrange them artistically in your garden. Don't forget to water them if it doesn't rain!

WHY NOT?
Fancy some mystery flora? When you next get home from a muddy walk, scrape the mud off the bottom of your boots and plant that. You'll be amazed at what might pop up!

DONE!

DATE COMPLETED

PLAY SAND DARTS

Are you a devil on the dartboard? Or maybe you've never played? Try this version the next time you're on the beach. Try to beat your best score!

1 Collect a pile of small pebbles and shells. These will be your "darts." (Avoid large and heavy pebbles or rocks that could hurt someone by mistake.)

2 Use your finger or one of the pebbles to draw a circle in the sand, about the width of your foot. Draw 4 bigger circles around that circle.

3 Mark the circles with the points you can earn for each ring: 10, 20, 30, 40, and 50 (for the "bull's-eye" in the center). Draw a line in the sand to stand behind for each throw.

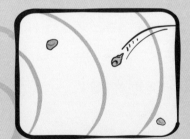

4 Take turns throwing your sand darts into the ring. Always throw underarm. Keep scores in the sand, and play to win!

DONE!

DATE COMPLETED

99 PLAY DROP CATCH

How good are you with a ball? Can you catch one on two knees, with one hand on the floor and both eyes closed?

1 Stand in a circle with some friends and space yourselves out equally. The farther apart you are, the more challenging the game will be. Decide who is going to start, and give that person the ball.

2 The first person should throw the ball to another player in the circle. If that player catches it, he or she then throws it to another player, and so on.

3 The ball is thrown back and forth in the circle until someone drops it. The "dropper" has to pay a penalty and continue to play on one knee. Any other "droppers" pay the same penalty.

4 If players on one knee catch their next ball, they can stand back up again. But if they drop that one too, they pay another penalty and go down on two knees. On a third drop, the player on two knees should also put one hand to the ground; on a fourth drop, close one eye; and on a fifth drop, close both eyes! If players with penalties catch the ball again, they can remove one penalty—for example, if they're on two knees, one knee can come up again. The last player still in the game wins!

DONE!

DATE COMPLETED

PLAY HORSE 100

You just need a basketball, a basketball hoop, and a group of friends to play this game. Who will spell HORSE first?

1 Stand in a line—this will be the order for you to take your turn. The first player takes a shot at the basketball hoop. If he or she makes the shot, then the second player has to make the same type of shot, from the same place as the first player.

2 If player 2 makes the shot, then the third player has to make the same shot, and so on. If player 2 misses, then he or she gets a letter—first H, then an O, and so on, until it spells HORSE. If players spell out the whole word, then they are out of the game.

3 When a player misses a shot, the next player gets to make up his or her own kind of shot that the others have to follow. Why not take a shot standing on one leg, or with your eyes closed?

4 Keep playing until there is only one player left—this person is the winner!

DONE!

DATE COMPLETED

101 MAKE AN OUTDOOR SILHOUETTE THEATER

Dusk and dark can be magical times outdoors. What better time to put on a shadow show for your family and friends? It can be quite simple . . . or simply epic!

YOU WILL NEED:

- An old sheet
- A big flashlight or outdoor lamp
- Sketch book and pencil
- Black card
- Scissors
- Split pins
- Barbecue sticks or a thin garden cane
- Masking tape
- Light-colored pencil or crayon
- Your imagination!

1 First, decide on the story that you are going to perform. Is it a well-known story, like a fairy tale? Or is it something you've made up yourself? Sketch the characters and props that you need.

2 Make your shadow puppets. For each character, draw a head and body onto the black card with the pencil or crayon. Include details, such as eyes, hair, and mouth.

3 Add limbs. Cut out arms and legs, and join them to your character's body with split pins. This will mean that you can move them in the show.

DONE! DATE COMPLETED

4 Attach the barbecue sticks to the main body and the limbs. Fix in place with the masking tape. You will hold the sticks to move the characters and their joints.

5 Hang the sheet up outside—you could tie it to the branches of a tree or between two posts. You will need space in front for the audience and behind for you to sit with the puppets. If you have nowhere to hang it, a couple of friends could hold the sheet for you.

6 Fix the light source. You could fix a big flashlight or outdoor lamp onto a tree or a post, or ask another friend to hold it for you.

7 Now invite your friends, wait until dark, and put on your show!

STAYING SAFE:
DOS AND DON'TS

 DO: Take care while using scissors and other sharp objects.

DO: Wear a helmet while riding a sled, bike, skateboard, etc.

DO: Always wear old clothes or an apron when doing art projects.

DO: Carefully follow the instructions and pay attention to any safety warnings.

DON'T: Start a messy project without asking an adult.

DON'T: Go anywhere without telling an adult first!

ACKNOWLEDGMENTS

Written by Susan Hayes
Design and illustration: Shahid Mahmood
Senior Designer: Katie Knutton
Senior Editor: Lydia Halliday
Editor: Fay Evans
Publisher: Donna Gregory

Fig. 67. *The Winchester/NRA Qualification Program provides a graduated program of achievement in a recreational shooting activity.*

Program consists of six different skill ratings which are earned by attaining the required scores on a series of increasingly challenging courses of fire. Shooting is done with two hands and within specific time limits to help build shooting skills having real-world applicability. The Winchester/NRA Handgun Qualification Program is a self-paced recreational shooting activity that provides shooters of all skill levels with both fun and a sense of accomplishment. For more information on the Winchester/NRA Handgun Qualification Program, see Appendix C: Facts About the NRA.

COMPETITION

Handgun competition is an excellent way to sharpen shooting skills, and the NRA offers matches open to beginner and expert alike. NRA Bullseye competition provides an opportunity to refine the shooting fundamentals—aiming, breath control, hold control, trigger control and follow-through—while NRA Action Pistol helps hone defensive skills by presenting varied target arrays that must be shot within relatively quick time limits. In most Action Pistol events, a large light-color target is used, with imprinted scoring rings in its center that are virtually invisible to the shooter. This helps the shooter develop the ability to accurately place shots in the center of target mass.

Practical handgun competition, such as that sponsored by IPSC

Fig. 68. *Match shooting helps sharpen gun handling and shooting skills under the pressure of competition.*

(International Practical Shooting Confederation), IDPA (International Defensive Pistol Association) and others, is a fun and exciting way to improve shooting and gun handling skills. In these sports, the shooter is presented with a virtually unlimited number of handgun challenges, and all firing is done against the clock. Most stages incorporate speed, movement and decision-making, thus giving the shooter practice in shooting accurately and quickly under stress.

For information on competing in NRA-sanctioned matches, as well as IDPA and IPSC competition, see Appendix B: Information and Training Resources.

ADDITIONAL TRAINING

The NRA Basic Personal Protection in the Home Course provides a thorough grounding in the fundamentals of defensive shooting and home protection. Extensive practice and rigorous application of the techniques introduced in this course will make the shooter interested in home protection more capable of defending his or her life and family.

Some shooters, however, may wish to obtain additional training to learn new shooting techniques or increase their proficiency in the techniques already learned. These individuals can avail themselves of the training available at numerous facilities throughout the country. Note that the instruction provided at such facilities may vary in terms of length, quality, type and cost.

Shooters contemplating enrolling at such a facility to enhance their skills should consider at least the following factors:

- reputation of facility
- geographic location
- cost
- credentials of instructors
- student-teacher ratio
- safety record of institution
- types of courses offered
- availability of nearby lodging (for multi-day courses)

EDUCATIONAL MATERIALS

In recent years there has been a great increase related to defensive shooting. Today's shooter ca hundreds of pamphlets, books and videos to gair every aspect of gun ownership and use, from ma to advanced firing techniques for self-defense an methods for the home. Appendix B: Information contains a sample of the available materials.

Fig. 69. This sample of NRA materials related to firearms, fi protection represents a small fraction of the materials curren You are urged to glean as much information as possible from including those outside the NRA, but always with a critical e safety of the techniques being taught.

Note that the NRA does not necessarily appr information contained in any of the materials lis much of the content of those materials is in agre training guidelines and policy, some content ma in NRA courses. You are urged to glean as much from a wide variety of sources, but always with effectiveness and safety of the techniques being

PART IV: STRATEGIES FOR HOME AND PERSONAL SAFETY

CHAPTER 13

MAKING YOU AND YOUR HOME SAFER

Regardless of your level of skill with a defensive firearm, it is always better—legally, morally, and practically—to *deter* or *evade* an attack or home intrusion rather than counter it with deadly force. No home can be made crime-proof, nor is there any personal strategy that will protect you from all threats under all conditions. However, there is much you can do to substantially decrease your risk of becoming a victim by making yourself and your home less attractive to a criminal and more difficult to attack. This is known as *reinforcing the target*.

MAKING YOURSELF SAFER

One of the first steps in making yourself safer is to ensure that you are projecting the proper image. The image you project often is the primary factor in whether or not a predatory criminal decides to target you as a victim. The way in which you carry yourself can either attract or deter a potential attacker. As the saying goes, "look like a sheep and you will be eaten by wolves."

Get into the habit of projecting a strong, confident demeanor during all of your activities, whether walking on the street, answering your door, or interacting with others, particularly strangers. Carry yourself erect with your chin up and shoulders back, and walk with a strong, confident and purposeful stride. When you approach or are approached by another person, momentarily look that person squarely in the eye so that they will know that you have seen them and are not intimidated by them. Do not, however, "lock eyes" with that person. After momentarily meeting the person's gaze, resume scanning the area to retain awareness of your surroundings and to avoid having your look misinterpreted as a challenge. With people of another race or culture, there may be various meanings attached to a direct, prolonged gaze into another person's eyes. In some cultures

Fig. 70. It is critical to present a strong and confident demeanor when confronting an attacker.

117

it is a sign of rudeness or intrusion, while in others it represents a threat that might provoke an angry or violent response. This may also be the case when encountering members of certain American subcultures, such as biker gangs, street gangs and others often spoiling for a fight, who will readily interpret your look as a challenge that must be answered.

When confronting those who come onto your property or invade your personal space, you should be especially forceful, purposeful, confident and energetic. Look the person squarely in the eye and act and speak with authority, using short, strong declarative sentences. If the person persists in violating your personal space, unobtrusively move away to maintain a buffer zone of safety. Make it clear to any person who intrudes on your space or property that you are in control of your environment, your household and your property—not the intruder.

While encountering a stranger who may represent a potential threat, it is common to feel a certain degree of nervousness or even fear. This is normal, and nothing to be ashamed of. The important factor is to control these feelings and not let them show to a potential adversary.

MAKING YOUR HOME SAFER

Increasing home security is accomplished by taking a number of different steps to make your residence less attractive to criminals, and to increase the difficulty of mounting a home intrusion or other attack.

A residence can be divided into several zones of security: grounds and landscaping, exterior of the home, interior of the home, and the safe room. Different steps can be taken within each zone to promote home security.

Grounds and Landscaping. When assessing the level of security provided by your yard and the vegetation it contains, it is beneficial to think like a criminal. You will probably see things in a vastly different light. The following are just a few of the many things you can do to make the area around your home less appealing to intruders.

Keep shrubs and other vegetation pruned below window level or so that it does not block the view from a window. Tree branches or bushes growing in front of windows can prevent you from looking out and seeing threats lurking outside. Also,

Fig. 71. This photo shows two security problems—vegetation under the windows that could provide a hiding place, and an air conditioner that could be pried out to allow entry.

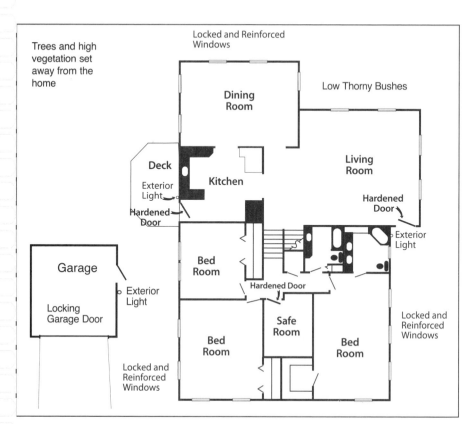

Fig. 72. A typical house and grounds, with a few of the steps that can be taken to make the home safer. As you progress inward through each security zone—grounds and landscaping, exterior of the home, interior of the home and the safe room—security should increase.

obstructing foliage can hide an intruder from the view of neighbors or passersby while he or she forces or breaks a window to gain access.

Trees and foliage that provide privacy from public view can also act as hiding-places for housebreakers. Consider reducing the number of trees or large bushes close to the home where they can provide a place from which an attacker may launch an ambush.

Consider planting thorny shrubs or other "unfriendly" plants to minimize an attacker's use of foliage as cover. Such plants should be located particularly around windows and other areas where you wish to discourage intruders.

Keep garage doors closed and remove remote door openers from vehicles. Preventing unauthorized access to the garage accomplishes a number of objectives. Most obviously, it prevents the theft of cars or other objects stored there. Most garages also contain tools of potential use to

Fig. 73. Vegetation near your home or garage can provide hiding places for potential attackers. Note also that the homeowner is in an "unaware" state regarding her surroundings.

home intruders, such as ladders, crowbars and hammers. An unlocked garage additionally may serve as a hiding place, giving an intruder more time to leisurely work on gaining entry, or may provide an ambush point for a violent attacker.

Change the factory-set access code of remote door openers to prevent unauthorized persons (such as the workmen who installed the system) from gaining access.

Avoid house designs featuring recessed entryways and other natural hiding places. If you are thinking of buying a house, avoid models whose architectural design

Fig. 74. Open garage doors can allow entry to an unwanted intruder.

provides ambush sites or hiding places for intruders. If you already own a house, assess your home for such areas and take whatever steps are necessary to minimize the danger. For example, avoid using recessed entryways at night, install lighting to thoroughly illuminate potential hiding places, and plant prickly or thorny bushes in alcoves and corners to discourage their use as ambush sites.

Avoid storing ladders, hammers, pry bars, screwdrivers or other tools having potential use to home intruders in outdoor sheds.

Keep outside lighting well maintained. Also, install lighting as needed to illuminate any areas close to the home that lie in darkness at night.

Maintain your level of awareness when approaching your house. Many people let their guard down when they turn into their driveway or go up their walk. Predators often know this, and take it into account when they plan their attacks.

Fig. 75. The area just around the corner (arrow) from this house's back door is a good ambush site for an assailant. At a minimum, lighting should be installed there to discourage would-be intruders. Steel bars should also be installed over the glass windows and door.

Fig. 76. This woman has relaxed her vigilance as she nears her front door (left), making her vulnerable to attack by an assailant hidden in nearby bushes.

When traveling, have a trusted friend or neighbor maintain a normal exterior appearance to your home. If you travel for an extended period, make sure your grass is cut regularly, your mail and newspapers are collected daily, your drapes or window blinds are repositioned occasionally, and any vehicles in your driveway are moved periodically.

Putting interior lights on staggered timers also gives the illusion of nighttime occupancy. In areas in which snow is to be expected, arrange to have your driveway plowed, your walk shoveled, and footprints to be made in the snow around your house. In this way, any burglars cruising your neighborhood for a potential target will assume that your house is currently occupied, and look elsewhere.

In connection with the above, do not reveal your travel plans to anyone who does not need to know them. Ensure that the neighbor or friend you select to maintain your home's lived-in appearance also preserves this necessary confidentiality.

Exterior of Home. An intruder who gains entry into you home does so by breaching the home exterior—doors, windows, and the like. Thus, it is critical to maintain the integrity of this zone.

Install quality steel doors, steel door frames, and door locks featuring both live- and deadbolts. Bolts should project at least 1" into the strike plate, and should have a hardened steel center pin that resists cutting. Strike plates can be reinforced by installing a substantial (1/8-inch thick or more) plate running from the top to the bottom of the door frame. Buy only quality locks designed to resist picking, prying or attack by blunt force; such locks are inexpensive insurance against easy entry.

Do not install pet doors. Juveniles and even small adults can pass through them, and they allow entry of tools used by a skilled housebreaker to unlock your doors. If you already have a pet door, close it permanently or replace the entire door.

Fig. 77. This 3/16-inch-thick steel plate reinforces the strike plate in the door frame.

Keep doors locked at all times. If your door, or the area around your door frame contains window panes, consider installing a deadbolt lock requiring a key on both sides. This will prevent a burglar from simply smashing the glass, reaching through and manually unlocking the door. If such a lock is used, however, you must keep a copy of the key in a specific place near the door to permit rapid exit in case of fire.

Consider the installation of a monitored alarm system. Such a system can result in a quick response to a break-in. Many have "panic buttons" that can be pushed to immediately alert authorities to the presence of an intruder. Non-monitored systems, which emit a piercing wail via an external horn or siren when security is breached, also can be useful to deter or scare away intruders. Even a sticker advertising that your home is protected by an alarm system is often sufficient to act as a deterrent.

Change locks when you first move in, lose a key, or suspect a key has been copied to prevent unauthorized access by former tenants, pickpockets or others. Also, periodically change the codes on remote door openers and keyless entry systems.

Close and lock ground floor windows in any rooms left unoccupied, or pin them so that they cannot be opened more than a few inches. Also, consider installing keyed window locks (to prevent a burglar from opening a window by simply breaking a pane and manually turning the lock).

Install steel bars spaced 4"-6" apart over windowpanes in the door or around the door frame to prevent an intruder from gaining entry by breaking the glass. Steel bars can also be put on ground-floor windows that are susceptible to forced entry. However, be sure that the bars do not hinder your fire evacuation plan.

Install wide-angle peepholes in all your exterior doors. Peepholes allow you to see who is at your door without opening the door. You can also use them to scan the identification of a police officer, repair person or others before you open the door.

Do not let strangers into your home for any reason. If someone requests assistance or needs to use your telephone, offer to make the call for them. When talking to strangers at night or under suspicious circumstances, converse through the door. Do not even crack the door open and thus give them the opportunity to push their way in,

Fig. 78. These steel bars prevent an intruder from gaining entry by simply breaking through the glass in the door. Keyed lock (arrow) prevents an intruder from reaching between the bars to unlock the door.

even if your door has a chain-type lock, as such locks are easily broken by a determined intruder.

Make repair persons, utilities representatives and others you may have to allow in your home show proper identification. If the person fails to show proper identification, do not let them in. If you feel their identification is questionable, call their employer and verify the individual's identification and need to enter your home. Often, repair persons coming to your home at your request (as to do work under a service contract) will be happy to set a specific appointment time, and/or call you enroute to your location.

Interior of Home. No matter what you do to the exterior of your home, you cannot absolutely prevent a home intruder from gaining entry if he or she is sufficiently determined. The level of motivation of a housebreaker depends in part upon how attractive a target your home appears to be. You can take a number of steps to make a criminal find your home less appealing and less vulnerable.

Do not place valuable articles where they can be seen through a window or door. Place electronic equipment, silverware, coin collections, valuable art or other similar items in rooms with visibility and security in mind. Stand at your own open front or back door and look into your home; what you see is what a stranger at your door will see.

If you must have strangers in your home—painters, appliance repair persons, utility representatives or the like—make sure that valuable objects are removed from, or at least hidden in, any areas such people must work in

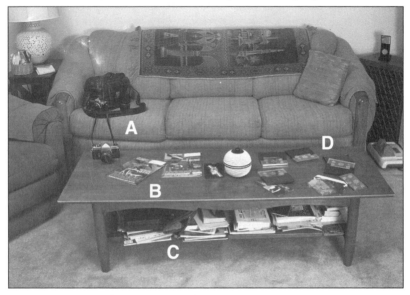

Fig. 79. On display in the room above are objects that may attract the attention of potential intruders such as (A) camera equipment, (B) gun magazines, (C) guns stored under the coffee table, and (D) items from a coin collection. Such objects should not be left out where they can be seen by a utility company worker, repair person, landlord, or any other stranger who may be given temporary access to your home.

or go through. Even if you have complete trust in the people who will be entering your home, they may innocently make a chance remark—"Gee, that guy at [insert your address here] sure has a lot of expensive camera gear"—to the wrong ears.

Keep firearms out of sight. Keep guns out of sight in a gun safe or vault, locked gun case, or other secure location. Also, store your gun safe, gun cases or other storage devices in a location unlikely to be seen by workers or other strangers who enter your home. If outsiders must enter the room in which your gun safe is located, try to disguise or conceal it with a screen, sheet or blanket. Gun safes—particularly small models that could easily be carried away by one or two people—should be bolted to the floor when possible.

Furthermore, take the same precautions with objects that tell a stranger you own guns. Do not leave gun magazines, books or videos, gun cleaning kits, or similar items lying around where they may be easily seen. If you are a hunter and have mounted trophies (heads, antlers, etc.), try to locate these in a room whose interior is not visible from any exterior doors or windows.

Window decals or bumper stickers that say "gun," such as a gun club membership sticker or even an NRA decal, should also be avoided.

Learn the location of all nooks, crannies, blind corners, shadowed areas and other natural hiding places in your home. This serves two purposes: first, to anticipate where you may unexpectedly confront an intruder; and second, to identify places that you or others in your family can use to escape attack (or surprise an intruder) if unable to get to the safe room.

To help with this process, mentally assume the role of an intruder and look around your home for places to hide or to surprise an unaware homeowner. Involve another family member in playing "hide and seek;" this is one of the best ways of discovering—and learning to anticipate— hiding places in the home. Of course, you must always perform these exercises without a firearm.

Practice walking around your home in the dark. Learn what floorboards, steps and doors creak, and what furniture is most likely to be bumped into. This practice will help you avoid making noise if you have to move around the house in darkness, and, more important, will facilitate the location of an intruder by listening to the sounds he or she makes while negotiating your house.

Make it seem as though you have a dog. If you actually own a dog, this is easy; simply make sure that evidence of the animal's presence—a chewed-up bone or toy, a large water or food dish, perhaps even a "Beware of the Dog" sign—is visible. If your dog is a small dog, buy him an oversized bowl and toy, and display these to make it seem as though you have a much larger animal.

If you do not own a dog, you should still obtain and display these items to create the impression in an intruder's mind that a large, angry watchdog may be lurking nearby.

If you do own a dog, make sure he is located so that, when he barks, you will hear and be warned by the sound, and a potential assailant will hear him as well. The deterrent effect of a dog depends largely upon an intruder hearing him give a warning bark.

THE SAFE ROOM

The safe room is like the keep of a medieval castle. It is your refuge when danger is present, and it is designed to protect you from a threat.

At least one room in the home should be designated a safe room. This room—usually the master bedroom—is carefully prepared to contain all the equipment necessary to maintain a defensive posture. In homes in which there are multiple adults in separate rooms, or small children, it may be advisable to establish more than one safe room. After retrieving a firearm and a phone, it may be appropriate for the adults in a family to retreat to the secondary children's safe room to protect them. Alternatively, one adult can stay in the primary safe room while another serves to protect the children in their safe room. In this scenario, both adults should be armed. Additionally, in large multi-story houses, it may be wise to establish safe rooms on more than one floor, in case an intruder cuts off your path to the primary safe room.

Whenever you establish more than one safe room—particularly on the same floor—you must establish lanes of fire that will not endanger any member of the household. If you are forced to shoot from your defensive position in the safe room, you will most likely fire at a target standing in the doorway of the room. This could present a danger to other members of your

Fig. 80. A family confronting a threat in their safe room. One adult has retrieved a firearm from a locked storage box while the other is using the telephone to contact the police. Note that the safe room is also equipped with a flashlight, and that each child has a designated, protected position in the room.

family if the secondary safe room is located right across the hall. In such a case, a bullet missing or passing through your target could penetrate the wall or door of the secondary safe room and injure someone inside. You must make similar allowances for the possible trajectory of an assailant's bullets.

Not just any room in your home can be a safe room. All effective safe rooms have certain characteristics in common, and contain certain basic items of equipment.

Reinforced. A safe room should be reinforced and fortified, if possible. This means that the room should have a solid door with a steel-reinforced frame and both live and deadbolt locks.

One Point of Entry. The safe room should have only a single point of entry—usually one door. This makes the room easier to defend. Note that a safe room should be located on an upper floor, if possible. The window in a ground-floor safe room could become a second point of entry, or could be fired through by your assailant or an accomplice.

Windows. The safe room should have one or more windows through which you can communicate with police when they arrive. Ideally, such a window should not be too high up, or you may find it difficult to communicate through.

If you decide to use a window for escape, be aware that you may be putting yourself in even greater danger by abandoning your safe room. The decision to escape through a window is one that must be made depending upon the situation.

If a window escape is incorporated into your defensive plan, be sure that any upper-level safe room contains a fire-escape-type ladder that hooks onto the window sill and extends down to the ground.

Equipment. Your safe room should contain, at the minimum, the following items:

• Telephone. Ideally, your telephone should have a lighted dial so that it can be dialed in the dark, and emergency numbers should already be entered into the phone's auto-dialer, if available. Any emergency number you must dial other than 911 should be written on a sticker and attached to the telephone. Your own street address and phone number should also be taped to the phone, so you can avoid giving the police dispatcher the incorrect information under stress. If possible, keep a cellular phone in the safe room as well, to ensure continuity of communication if your normal phone lines are cut, or if the intruder

Fig. 81. Your safe room should have a telephone with emergency numbers taped to it.

picks up an extension on your regular phone line to prevent you from dialing out.

• Police-style flashlight and fresh batteries. This type of flashlight normally has a durable, heavy aluminum body, a switch designed for many on-off cycles, and a bright, focusable beam. Such a flashlight can also be used as a last-ditch defensive club should your firearm jam or you run out of ammunition. Test the batteries in your flashlight periodically, and keep a fresh set of batteries with your flashlight.

Fig. 82. An aluminum-bodied police-style flashlight is rugged and durable, and can be used as a club if necessary.

• Firearm and ammunition. Your personal protection firearm should always be in the safe room. During a home intrusion, you cannot count on being able to retrieve a gun and ammunition from a separate location and take it with you as you withdraw to the safe room. You may not be able to remember where your gun and ammunition are located, or you may not have time to go and get them. Moreover, depending upon where an intruder enters your home, you may be cut off from a defensive gun that is not located in your safe room.

Your decision of how to store your safe room firearm depends upon a number of factors, including the presence or absence of children or others in your household not authorized to handle firearms, the level of endemic threat in your neighborhood, and, of course, any state or local laws mandating firearm storage methods. Many of the same factors, as well as the method of storage you select, will influence your decision about whether or not to keep the stored firearm in a loaded condition.

You should also keep extra loaded magazines or extra loaded speedloaders and a spare box of ammunition in the safe room.

• Items Providing Cover. Your defensive position in the safe room should make use of items capable of protecting you from an assailant's

Fig. 83. If a firearm is part of your personal protection strategy, it should be kept in a storage device in the safe room, along with spare magazines.

bullets, such as a water bed, a heavy steel filing cabinet, a filled bookcase (positioned so that bullets would traverse it lengthwise) or a heavy solid wood dresser filled with clothes. If possible, equip the safe room with items providing cover if such items are not already there. Be sure to at least have cover for any children who may take refuge in the safe room.

Position your cover so that it provides protection from the likely field of fire of your assailant. Also, do not place cover in a location in which people hiding behind it could be exposed to an errant shot from your gun.

If you are unable to provide cover for all of the occupants of the safe room, at least make sure that there is adequate concealment for all occupants.

Fig. 84. All persons in the safe room should take advantage of cover and concealment as much as possible. Note protected position of adult using telephone.

• Extra set of house keys attached to a large reflector, a fluorescent glow-stick or simply a piece of wood. This is thrown out of your safe room window to the responding officers after contact has been established with them, to permit their easy entry into your home. This set of keys should be kept in a location easily accessed in the dark, such as on a hook hidden behind window curtains.

• Dark colored sweat pants and T-shirt. If you sleep in minimal

Fig. 85. A set of house keys attached to a light-colored piece of wood can be thrown out the safe room window to permit the police easy entry to your home.

clothing, you may want to have additional clothing in the safe room. If you are roused from sleep by a suspicious sound and retreat to the safe room, such additional clothing may allow you to greet the responding police without embarrassment.

The recommended dark clothing serves more than just to preserve modesty. Safe room occupants with light skin should attempt to cover as much of their skin as possible to increase their concealment from an assailant in a dark safe room.

FLEEING THE SAFE ROOM

Although withdrawal to a safe room is generally considered the most prudent course of action when dealing with a potential or real threat in the home, you should always be alert to any opportunity to evade or escape the threat. Flight, *if it can be undertaken safely*, should always be considered the most preferable course of action. It is better to simply leave your house and avoid a confrontation altogether than to remain in the safe room and have to use lethal force to survive.

However, it must be added that in many, if not most, cases the option of safe flight will not be available to you. For example, if you are uncertain regarding the exact location, number or intentions of the intruders, an attempt to flee could put you into a position of even greater danger. Also, flight could be problematic when there are small children or a bedridden or wheelchair-bound family member. It is imperative that an escape plan be formulated well before a potential confrontation arises, and practiced by every member of the family. An important part of this escape plan is to establish the conditions determining whether flight, or withdrawal to the safe room, is the preferred plan of action.

Fig. 86. Although withdrawing to your safe room is generally the most prudent course of action, simply fleeing your home should be considered if it can be done safely. Flight may not be safe, however, when there is uncertainty about the number and location of the assailants. Under such circumstances, flight may actually expose you to greater risk, as in the above scenario, in which a woman fleeing out her back door to escape an assailant inside her house encounters an accomplice waiting outside.

CHAPTER 14

RESPONDING TO A POSSIBLE BREAK-IN

Much of this book deals with developing the skills, mindset and defensive plan to deal with an imminent violent encounter. You also must prepare for situations in which you are faced with only a potential threat, rather than an actual one. A potential threat, such as a possible home intrusion, must be taken extremely seriously, as it may easily and unexpectedly turn into an immediate, life-threatening attack. This chapter deals with your response to a possible intrusion—a situation in which a threat is suspected but has not been confirmed, and there is no face-to-face confrontation with an intruder.

Because of the uncertainty of a situation in which the threat is ambiguous or unclear, responding to a possible break-in requires as much defensive planning as when the threat is real and clearly defined. Your family's plan for a possible home intrusion should be coordinated and comprehensive, just like your plan for evacuating your home in the event of a fire. Also, just as members of your household perform fire drills to reinforce the evacuation plan, your plan for responding to a potential threat also should be regularly practiced.

At the very least, your plan should incorporate the following steps: withdraw to safety, secure the safe room, call the police, and issue a verbal warning if the intruder approaches the safe room. In addition, you must also pre-determine the actions you will take to make contact with and greet the police when they arrive.

WITHDRAW TO SAFETY

The first action you should take when an intruder is suspected is withdraw to safety. This means that you and the various members of your household must immediately go to the primary or secondary safe room (provided the threat does not lie on the route to the safe room). Any family members who are already in the safe room should stay there.

You and your family will have to determine what stimuli, actions or events constitute a potential threat and justify a retreat to the safe room and the summoning of police officers. Suspicious sounds (such as the breaking of window or door glass, or the sound of footsteps in your home when you are alone) are often a good indicator. A sudden loss of telephone and electric power service, with no storm or other apparent cause, might also warn you of an impending home intrusion.

Many incidents that might be indicative of a break-in, however, may

also have innocent origins. Everyone has had the experience of being startled by the sudden slamming of a door or rattling of a window, only to realize that it was just the wind that blew the door shut or caused a tree branch to tap against a windowpane. In many instances the significance of a given noise or event will be unclear, and you or other members of your household will have to interpret it to the best of your ability.

You will also have to establish some signal to warn other household members of the presence of a potential threat and the need to retreat to the safe room. This could be a bell, buzzer or other alarm system—activated by a household member pushing a button or throwing a switch—or simply the yelled words, "Safe room—NOW!" Note that any electronic alarm must be able to be activated in any part

Fig. 87. When an adult or other authorized person gives the pre-established signal, such as a bell, buzzer, or simply the words, "Safe room—NOW!", all members of the family should immediately go to the safe room.

of the house, for it cannot be predicted where a potential threat may appear.

While it might be argued that any such signal will also warn the intruder that he or she has been detected, the supposed disadvantage of this probably will be outweighed by the importance of alerting household members of the need to immediately retreat to safety. Also, in some cases the sudden sounding of an alarm will deter a criminal and cause him or her to flee.

Electronic alarm systems that automatically sound when a door is opened or a window is broken can be useful in alerting family members to any breach in the defensive home exterior. However, there may be potential intrusion situations that will not be signaled by the alarm system. Members of the household should not rely wholly upon that system, but should remain alert to all types of indications that may signal a home intrusion.

It has been stated that every family member should immediately retreat to the safe room when confronted with a suspicious stimulus or a prearranged signal. Before going to the safe room, however, each person should take the time—a second or two at most—to turn off or unplug any appliance or tool that might create a safety hazard if left unattended, such as a propane torch, steam iron or oven. It is counterproductive to set your house on fire as a result of seeking safety from a burglar.

Fig. 88. On the way to the safe room, each person should take a second or two to turn off any appliance or tool that could create a hazard if left on unattended.

There may be a need to develop contingency plans for members in different areas of your home, in case their path to the safe room brings them toward the potential threat. If you are alone in your home and working in your basement, for example, and hear suspicious footsteps on the first floor, it would be foolish for you to go upstairs, toward a possible attacker, to seek the protection of a second-floor safe room. Your contingency plan may include fleeing your home through a basement door or window, or retreating to a secondary safe room in your basement. As mentioned in the previous chapter, in a large, multi-story home, it may be advisable to establish a separate, carefully chosen safe room or area on each floor.

Fig. 89. Each family member in the safe room should have an assigned position behind cover.

In the safe room, each household member should have a designated safe spot to retreat to. In some cases, as with small children, it may also be advisable to specify a particular posture as well (for example, head down, eyes closed and hands over their ears). It is essential that each person remain in his or her designated spot until the emergency is over.

Under no circumstances

Fig.90. Searching your home for an attacker may expose you to greater risk.

should you or any other household member conduct a search for a potential intruder; the probability of being ambushed is far too high. Even for trained professionals, searching for a hidden and potentially armed intruder entails great risk. If you search for an intruder, all he needs to do is stay still and quiet in a hidden position, such as behind a chair or around a corner, and wait for you to come to him. He will be forewarned of your approach by the sounds you make or the shadow you cast, while you won't have a clue as to his location. Your odds are better if you stay still and quiet in your safe room, and force the intruder to do the searching.

SECURE THE SAFE ROOM

Once all family members who can safely do so have retreated to the safe room and have assumed their designated positions, the safe room door should be closed and locked and the defensive firearm should be retrieved and loaded (if it is not already loaded). Normally, one family member will be assigned to handle the defensive firearm. In addition, the telephone and flashlight (if appropriate) must be retrieved and readied for use. This might involve removing the telephone from a nightstand and placing it on the floor next to your defensive position behind the bed so that you can use it without exposing yourself to hostile fire any more than necessary.

After securing the safe room, simply listen for any more suspicious sounds. If you do not immediately hear any noise, wait and listen for at least 15 minutes more. Do not be quick to assume there is no danger; it is better to listen a few minutes more and be that much more certain that no threat exists or remains. Remember that an intruder may be playing the same waiting game, figuring that if you don't hear any additional noise you will assume that all is safe and leave the protection of your safe room.

If you hear any suspicious sound or observe any suspicious circumstance, such as the electric power suddenly going out, call the police immediately.

Assuming you do not discern anything suspicious after waiting at least 15 minutes, you and your family may leave the safe room. You may feel a bit sheepish at this point. After all, everyone in your household abandoned what they were doing, became frightened or excited, and wasted a quarter of an hour or more—and all for nothing. However, it is better to withdraw to safety and continue the rest of your emergency plan (even when it turns out you did not need to do so) than to ignore early warning signs of danger and be tragically victimized. Learn to trust your instincts.

CALL THE POLICE

You must call the police immediately if you hear any suspicious sounds or note any suspicious circumstances after you have retreated to the safe room. Most areas have a 911 emergency phone number; if your area has this, use it. If you must dial some other number for police or other emergency services, be sure to have that number written on a sticker or label attached to the telephone in your safe room. That label should also contain your own address and telephone number.

Tell the emergency operator that you think someone has broken into your home. Give the operator your name and address and tell him or her where you and other family members are in the house, and that you are armed.

Once you have given the above information to the emergency operator, do not hang up. Remain on the line until the police arrive on the scene and you establish verbal contact with them.

If the intruder approaches the part of your house where you are hiding, you will have to shift focus from talking to the emergency operator to dealing with the intruder. Put the telephone down and prepare to defend yourself,

Fig. 91. After calling the police in your safe room, do not disconnect the line but leave the phone where you can easily access it and where the dispatcher can hear what is going on in the room.

but do not hang up the telephone. All 911 calls (and most other emergency calls) are recorded. If you are forced to shoot an aggressor in self-defense, the 911 recording of the encounter could later prove crucial to your legal defense.

ISSUE A VERBAL WARNING

If the intruder is outside the door to the safe room, or is attempting to gain entry to the room, yell a verbal warning: "Get out! The police are on their way. I have a gun. I'll shoot if you come in." This warning should be said forcefully, purposefully, and above all, loudly. A verbal warning does little good if it is not heard, and a loud, forceful warning is more intimidating than one delivered in normal voice tones. Also, remember that you are being recorded on the emergency telephone line. A warning that is yelled is more likely to be recorded clearly, and will support your claim of justifiable self-defense, should you be forced to shoot.

If the intruder succeeds in gaining access to the safe room, you will have to defend yourself. This subject is discussed in detail in Chapter 15: Confronting an Intruder or Attacker and Chapter 16: If You Must Shoot.

WHEN THE POLICE ARRIVE

When law enforcement officers are called to respond to a possible break-in, they do not know what they will find when they arrive. They might find nothing at all. Or they may encounter injured or dead victims, a hostage situation, a violent former spouse, or even an armed psychopath who made the call to lure police officers into a deadly ambush. Given the possibilities, it is to be expected that the responding officers will be highly alert, tense, and ready to defend themselves. Your behavior toward them in the first few minutes after they arrive will determine their perception of you, and set the tone for the interaction you have with them.

Making Contact with Police on the Scene. When the police arrive, stay where you are. Remember, the police do not know who might be a home owner or a burglar. The emergency operator can act as a link between you and the officers at the scene. Tell the operator again where you are in the house and that you are armed. Describe your appearance and clothing to the operator, as well as that of any other household member who may be encountered by the police (such as a family member in a secondary safe room).

Through the emergency operator, direct the police to the area outside your safe room window and tell them you are going to throw out a house key attached to a reflector. Make sure this message has been relayed to the police officers; a person unexpectedly showing up at a window with a shiny object in his or her hand will cause concern among the officers. Do not appear at the window with a gun in your hand. Put your gun down first. Also, tell the police where in your home you suspect the intruder might be located.

Police Entry. The police will use your house key to enter your house. If they are equipped with a K-9 unit (police dog), they may send the dog in first. Warn the police as to the location or presence of other household members not in the safe room, or the presence of family pets.

Stay in the locked safe room until you are directed by the police to come out. This is particularly important if a police dog has entered the house. The

Fig. 92. When the police arrive, throw a set of house keys, mounted on a large reflector or paddle, out of the window to allow them entry.

dog will attack anyone in the house, whether an intruder or household member. If you are confronted by a police dog, do not move!

Greeting the Police. Once the police have satisfied themselves that there are no intruders in the house, they will make verbal contact with you through the door of your safe room. Wait in the safe room until you are told to come out. Do not emerge with a gun in your hand or anywhere on your person. Put your gun down in a spot well away from the door.

When directed to do so, open the door to the safe room and come out slowly with your empty hands in plain sight. Do exactly what the police tell you to do.

Do not be surprised if the police frisk you or otherwise treat you as though you were a suspect. To the police, who are walking into an unknown situation, you are a suspect until your identity is established. Be sympathetic if the officers initially treat you with suspicion and skepticism.

Fig. 93. Greet the police with your hands in plain sight; your firearm should be unloaded and not in your hand.

CHAPTER 15

CONFRONTING AN INTRUDER OR ATTACKER

The preceding chapters contain a variety of strategies and steps to deter, prevent or escape a criminal attack. Even when these are observed, however, you may still be forced to come face to face with an intruder or attacker. You may be taken by surprise and cut off from your safe room, or confronted by an intruder who unexpectedly breaks down your door. Even if you are in your safe room, you may still have to repel an attacker who refuses to be deterred.

You must be prepared—through training, prior visualization and mentally playing out scenarios—to be in control of the situation and act decisively. You must be prepared to use deadly force if your assailant presents an imminent deadly threat.

CONTROLLING THE ENCOUNTER

When you find yourself face-to-face with an intruder, your first and most important concern is to stay as far away from him as possible. Do not be misled by the intruder's demeanor. Even if he seems to be unarmed and compliant, he may suddenly attack you if you let him get close enough.

When giving an intruder instructions, yell your commands as loud as you can. This will both intimidate him and will help overcome his auditory exclusion (explained later in this chapter). Do not converse or reason with your attacker. He will often attempt to gain your sympathy, to appeal to your good nature, or to convince you that you have made a mistake in suspecting him of any criminal intent. He may try to convince you to let him go; he may even approach you slowly, talking softly and reasonably. Do not be fooled by this behavior. You must remain in control of the situation. If an intruder flees, let him go. If an intruder continues to approach you and refuses to stop, you must defend yourself appropriately.

If you have taken him by surprise and are able to hold him for the police, do not approach him or attempt to frisk him. If he has a weapon, have him carefully place it on the ground (muzzle pointing away from you if it is a firearm). Make sure his hands stay visible to you at all times. Have him lie face-down on the floor, away from his weapon, chin on the floor and legs spread apart, with his hands held palms-up and stretched straight out from his shoulders.

While you are holding the intruder for the police, you must also remain

alert to any other intruders you have not detected. If possible, seek cover with your back against the wall, or otherwise position yourself so that you can cover the intruder while protecting yourself from surprise attack. Call the police, and never take your eyes off your attacker.

Note that any intruder you are holding at gunpoint has three choices: run away, comply with your commands, or attack you and get shot. If he chooses flight, let him go.

Fig. 94. When you hold an attacker for the police, back against a wall and make him lie face down, facing away from you, with the palms upward.

PSYCHOLOGICAL REACTIONS TO A THREATENING ENCOUNTER

The body responds in a number of ways to being threatened with bodily harm. For example, the parts of the brain that control higher thought processes begin to shut down, relinquishing control to more primitive, survival-oriented brain centers.

Every life-threatening encounter is different, and each person responds to an attack in a different way. There is no way to determine ahead of time how a person will react to a particular situation, even if that person has been in a similar situation before.

When confronted with an attack, you may initially delay responding because of denial—you just can't believe that you are being assaulted. Also, many people have an internal resistance to inflicting deadly force on another person in a face-to-face encounter. This inherent reluctance can be overcome through fear, as well as through conditioning and visualization training.

There are five possible responses to any life-threatening encounter: *freeze, submit, posture, flight* or *fight.*

The Basics of Personal Protection in the Home

Freeze. The victim of an attack may be so overwhelmed or surprised by being threatened that he or she may freeze and become incapable of any action whatsoever. A momentary freeze resulting from confusion, shock, initial panic or denial of what is occurring is normal and, in fact, should be expected. In some cases, however, the frozen state may persist throughout the duration of the encounter.

Submit. Submission is simply giving in to an attacker. While it is often said that one should accede to an assailant's demands so as not to antagonize him into further violence, there is research indicating that a person defending his or her life with a firearm is less likely to be injured by fighting back than by submitting.

There may be occasions when submission seems the prudent course of action, such as when you are at a serious practical disadvantage (for example, when you are completely unarmed) and an armed assailant appears more interested in relieving you of your valuables than your life. However, it is impossible to predict the outcome of a potentially violent situation, particularly when you are relying upon the good will of a criminal. Crime statistics show that present-day criminals are more willing than their predecessors to maim or kill needlessly, even when the robbery or burglary victim is completely compliant. Seemingly pointless murders have been committed to gain status within a gang, silence or intimidate witnesses, or simply for the thrill of killing. Thus, the risk of inciting your attacker to greater violence by resisting must be weighed against the danger of putting yourself at the mercy of his or her whims if you submit. Choosing between those alternatives depends upon your moment-to-moment assessment of the situation.

Even under the best of circumstances, submission is never a safe choice. Proper preparation involving training, the defensive mindset, and the development of an effective defensive plan reduces the likelihood of being caught in a situation in which submission seems the best alternative.

Posture. Posturing is combat without contact. Words, sounds, gestures and body language are the weapons used to dominate, intimidate and subdue another. Posturing is frequently seen in the animal world when members of the same species growl, paw the ground, make mock charges and otherwise exhibit aggressive behavior that stops short of actual fighting. Such showdowns usually

Fig. 95. An assailant posturing in an attempt to intimidate his intended victim.

end with the retreat or submission of one of the animals.

Humans frequently engage in similar behavior. Depending upon the circumstances of the encounter, both attacker and victim may attempt to out-bluster each other until one backs down or flees.

Flight. Flight, also known as retreat, involves removing yourself from the source of the threat. Flight or retreat is a natural instinct when confronted with danger. In some defensive situations, it will not be possible to retreat without the risk of incurring injury.

Fight. In a self-defense context, the fight response involves the use of whatever force is reasonable and necessary to prevent harm from an attacker. Deadly force may be used only when there is an imminent threat of severe harm or death.

Obviously, not every victim of a violent attack will experience all or even most of the above-mentioned psychological reactions. Nor can you predict how you will react in a given situation. It is not uncommon to experience an escalating series of responses—for example, from freeze to flee to posture and finally fight.

Do not forget that your attacker probably will experience the same psychological reactions. A burglar you surprise, for example, may initially freeze, then posture in an attempt to bluff his way out of the situation. When this fails, he may simply flee. Your attacker very likely has one or more contingency plans for a potential confrontation before he has even entered your home. This will give him an advantage over you if you have not developed similar plans.

PHYSIOLOGICAL REACTIONS TO A LIFE-THREATENING ENCOUNTER

No matter what your level of training or how capable you believe yourself to be in handling stressful situations, you will experience, to a greater or lesser degree, a number of involuntary physiological changes during a serious defensive situation.

General Bodily Responses to Imminent Danger. In most cases, there will be a period of time between when you first perceive a threat and an attack actually occurs. This may occur, for example, when you awaken to hear an intruder breaking in downstairs. During this period you probably will experience a number of bodily responses to imminent danger. Your heart rate and respiration will increase (to provide more blood and oxygen to the muscles and brain), your pupils will dilate (to take in more light and see the threat better), and your muscles will be tighter in anticipation of sudden movement.

Adrenaline Rush. One of the ways your body prepares you for flight or fight is through the release of the hormone adrenaline into your bloodstream. This powerful chemical heightens the senses and increases strength, and can also cause trembling of the muscles. This trembling can make it more difficult to stand or sit still or, more important, to hold the firearm steady. This trembling can be mistaken for fear by both the assailant and victim. In reality, it is a physical reaction to the excess of adrenaline that has been dumped into the bloodstream in preparation for an attack. This is also what causes the uncontrollable shaking sometimes experienced after a confrontation is over: the body is no longer utilizing all the adrenaline that was released.

Note that although the heightened awareness caused by adrenaline may enable you to more readily perceive a threat, it may also predispose you to overreact to any sudden stimulus.

Loss of Fine Motor Skills. Stress—regardless of its source—results in a loss of fine motor skills. This is often experienced in daily life. For example, it is much harder to unlock your front door with a key when you are rushing to get to a ringing telephone inside. In sports, too, it is common for many athletes to perform better in practice than under the stress of actual competition.

During an attack, your loss of fine motor control will manifest itself in many ways. For example, you will find it more difficult to load cartridges into a pistol magazine or revolver cylinder, or to work the combination lock on a gun box or gun safe. To compensate for this loss of fine motor control, the NRA Personal Protection in the Home Course teaches gun handling skills that involve gross motor skills only. This is also why well-designed defensive handguns are simple to operate, and feature controls that are easily and naturally actuated by large muscle movements.

PERCEPTUAL CHANGES DURING A THREATENING ENCOUNTER

Survivors of violent attacks—as well as those who have experienced certain other extremely stressful situations—commonly report that, during the attack or stressful event, their perceptions of visual and auditory stimuli, as well as the passage of time, were altered. These alterations—tunnel vision, auditory exclusion and time dilation—are involuntary, and may have evolved as a survival mechanism to better focus all of one's senses and concentration on an immediate source of danger. While these perceptual changes may have worked extremely well in enabling our ancestors to fight saber-toothed tigers, they do not always provide as much of a benefit when dealing with one or more intelligent, determined human assailants.

Tunnel Vision. Under the stress of an imminent or actual attack, you will be focused almost exclusively on the perceived threat, and will be virtually oblivious to anything going on elsewhere in your visual field. This phenomenon is known as *tunnel vision*.

Learn to search for additional threats by developing certain training habits (such as lowering the firearm and assessing the area after firing at a target). It is important to scan and assess during a defensive shooting situation. Not doing so could cause you to fail to recognize additional threats (or innocent persons) that may lurk just outside your immediate field of view.

Fig. 96. Tunnel vision can cause you to focus only on the threat, and thus keep you from seeing things outside your immediate field of view (such as the children in the background).

Auditory Exclusion. During a violent encounter you will also undergo *auditory exclusion*, a condition during which extraneous sounds may be inaudible. Sounds emanating from outside your visual perception—and even those from within it—may go unheard. People involved in shootings often report that the sound of their own gunshots was no louder to them than a popgun.

You can at least partially counteract the effects of auditory exclusion by screaming your commands to your assailant. Not only does this help break through the veil of auditory exclusion; it also serves to intimidate him.

Keep in mind that you will not be the only one suffering auditory exclusion; your assailant as well as any family members, police officers or innocent bystanders who may be involved in the situation will experience it as well.

Time Dilation. *Time dilation* refers to the perception of slowed time that occurs during extreme stress. You may see the movements of both your assailant and yourself as happening in slow motion, and you lose the ability to accurately determine the passage of time. A few seconds of actual time may seem to you to be much longer in duration. The phenomenon of time dilation is the reason why, when you are first alerted to strange sounds or other early warnings of a potential threat, you should wait much longer than you may initially think is necessary before you relax your guard or emerge from hiding.

CHAPTER 16

IF YOU MUST SHOOT

As emphasized repeatedly throughout this book, a firearm is a *tool of last resort* in dealing with a violent encounter. Whenever possible and safe, *it is always preferable to prevent, deter, evade or escape an attack.* Unfortunately, there are times when these options are not available, and you must use whatever means are at your disposal—including your defensive firearm—to stop an attack and protect your life or the lives of loved ones.

There is nothing—no shooting sport, no motion picture or instruction manual, and no training regimen—that can fully prepare you for the experience of using your defensive firearm against a violent assailant. Nonetheless, those gun owners who avail themselves of every opportunity to prepare mentally and physically for a defensive situation will almost always fare better than those who don't. A large part of this preparation involves understanding what actually goes on during and after a shooting.

ART DOESN'T ALWAYS IMITATE LIFE

Most people in our society have little or no experience with shooting situations. For many, television and motion pictures are the primary source of information regarding guns and gunfights. Regrettably, the portrayals of firearm use in these media bear little resemblance to what actually occurs in real life. Knowing the difference between firearm fact and firearm fiction will enable you to better handle a defensive shooting situation.

Perhaps the greatest misconception fostered by the media lies in the effects of being shot. When a character is shot in motion pictures or television shows, the bullet strike produces a large, explosively bloody, easily-seen entrance wound and throws the person violently backward. Often a single shot causes instantaneous collapse.

In reality, this depiction is almost completely inaccurate. Both participants in and witnesses to handgun shootings typically report an inability to spot bullet strikes. Also, a bullet hit often produces no discernible effect whatsoever—certainly not the violent backward motion exhibited by shooting victims in the entertainment media. Furthermore, studies of shooting incidents show that situations in which one-shot stops or instantly incapacitates an assailant are the exception rather than rule. More commonly, multiple shots from a handgun are required to stop an attacker.

This last point cannot be overemphasized. Even when the first shot is well-placed in the center of mass, incapacitation usually results only after several shots—and several seconds. Hitting a vital organ on your assailant, such as the heart or lungs, may not immediately cause a cessation of the attack, particularly if he or she is under the influence of alcohol or drugs, or is highly motivated to do you harm or take your life. Even when the heart stops, sufficient fresh oxygen remains in the brain and muscles to continue activity for up to 30 seconds—more than enough time for an aggressor to shoot, stab, club or even strangle you. You should assume that your first shot will not immediately stop an attack. This is one of the reasons you need to continue to fire at the assailant until there is no longer any imminent deadly threat.

While there are areas on the body where a bullet hit will produce instant incapacitation, they are very small and unlikely to be hit even by an experienced shooter under the stress and rapid movement of a violent encounter. A solid center of mass hit (or hits) is the surest way to stop an attack quickly.

In television or motion-picture gunfights, little concern is given to the consequences of a shot that misses its target. In the media, misses simply splatter against nearby cover or ricochet away harmlessly. In the real world, bullets that miss their targets have to go somewhere, and in a thin-walled house or apartment they may cause injury to innocent bystanders. Even bullets that ricochet can fly great distances and cause serious harm. Unlike your favorite action hero, you must be aware of where every bullet you fire can go— including misses.

It is interesting that in many action movies, the hero or heroine almost always drops dozens of opponents with but a single shot each, while the bad guys always seem to miss or produce only wounding hits. Like so many of the media portrayals of

Fig. 97. In real life, a bullet can inflict injury on innocent bystanders in the event of a miss, or if it completely penetrates the intended target. Be aware of persons around or behind your target.

firearm use, the implicit message in such movies—that the good guys always shoot better than the bad guys—is a fantasy.

LIKELIHOOD OF INJURY

As discussed above, the great majority of assaults take place at very close range—often a matter of only a few feet. It has also been pointed out that an attacker is unlikely to be stopped immediately with a single shot. Several shots and several seconds may be required until an assailant no longer presents a threat. These two facts, plus the possibility of encountering multiple assailants, create a strong likelihood that you will suffer some degree of injury during an attack.

For example, it has been shown that an assailant wielding a knife even as far away as seven yards—21 feet—can usually get to and injure an armed defender before that defender can stop him with a handgun. This is often known as the *21-foot rule*. Since most attacks take place at ranges considerably less than seven yards, you can see that an attacker armed with no more than a knife or club (or even his bare hands) often will be able to wound an armed defender.

The probability of being injured while defending yourself from attack should not, however, deter you from exercising your right of self-defense. Some misguided people believe that resisting an attack makes it more likely that you will be injured. U.S. Justice Department studies show that people who resist an assailant do, indeed, suffer a greater likelihood of injury than those who comply—*except for those who resist with a firearm.* In these studies, armed citizens who used a gun to protect their lives were

Fig. 98. At close distance, a determined attacker using a knife will likely be able to inflict some injury to the home defender, even if she achieves several good hits from her pistol.

considerably less likely to be injured than those who did not fight back. Simply put, if you cannot prevent, deter, evade or escape a violent attack, the effective use of a defensive firearm represents your best choice for minimizing your chances of injury or death.

There are several methods by which you can lessen the likelihood of injury from a violent assailant. The use of cover can protect you from not only an attacker's bullets but also from any other weapon wielded against you. In any defensive situation, you need to create as much distance as possible between yourself and a violent criminal. This may take you out of the range of contact of edged weapons, and decreases the probability of being hit by shots fired by an assailant. Creating distance also means that you do not delay firing upon an approaching aggressor. As discussed above, a determined assailant starting from 7 yards away (a distance longer than most rooms in the average house) will almost certainly reach you before you can stop him, even with multiple gunshots. You must not wait to fire upon an approaching aggressor until the last possible moment in the hope that he will have a change of heart. You should fire whenever there is an unavoidable and immediate threat to life or limb—whether that threat is at arm's length or across the room.

Combining the use of both cover and distance can give you more time to react and can place obstacles between you and your assailant. These obstacles—chairs, tables, doors and so forth—will slow down your attacker, giving you more time to react and deliver accurate fire, if necessary.

IF YOU ARE INJURED

Even if you sustain an injury during an attack, it is essential to keep fighting. The indomitable will to prevail is the single most important factor in ensuring your survival in a deadly encounter.

Keep in mind that an initial wound from a knife, a club or even a handgun is not likely to be fatal. If you stop fighting when you are first injured, however, you likely will receive additional, possibly lethal injuries. You must always keep fighting, no matter how badly you think you are hurt. The sooner you stop your attacker, the fewer injuries you or your loved ones will receive, and the faster medical attention can be obtained for all injured parties.

To help you deal with the possibility of being wounded during an attack, use mental preparation to help strengthen your resolve to prevail. To some degree, you can control how you react emotionally to situations; practice previsualizing yourself during an attack, receiving wounds and yet continuing to fight and prevail. Remember that many wounds look worse than they really are, due to copious bleeding, and that many survivors who were wounded in violent attacks report that they did not feel pain or otherwise realize that they were stabbed or shot until later, after the attack was over. In many of the cases in which victims were oblivious to the injuries they sustained, it was because they were completely focused mentally on the struggle to survive and win.

ONCE THE ATTACKER IS DOWN

If you are forced to shoot an attacker, you should follow specific procedures to ensure your safety and the safety of loved ones or other

Fig. 99. Immediately after firing shots at an assailant that stop his or her attack (left), you should lower your firearm slightly (right). This will allow you to break tunnel vision and to see the effect of your shots. Your finger should remain on the trigger so that you can quickly fire additional shots if necessary.

innocent bystanders. The most important rule to remember is that once your attacker is down, you must not approach him under any circumstances. Do not approach your attacker to disarm him, to check on his condition, to render first aid or for any other reason.

Immediately after you fire shots at an assailant that stop the attack, lower your firearm slightly, to break tunnel vision and to allow you to see the effect of your shots. Also, shift your eyes slightly from side to side to scan the area for additional assailants, but do not lose sight of your primary attacker.

At the same time, move to cover if you have not already done so. Reload your handgun if its ammunition supply has been depleted. Although it may seem that the danger has passed once your assailant is down and seemingly incapacitated, it is just as important to seek cover after shooting stops as before it starts. Remember, just because an attacker is down does not mean that he is no longer a threat. Even when wounded and on the ground, an assailant may still have the capability and the will to shoot, stab, punch or otherwise threaten you. Additionally, you may be confronted by a second hidden assailant.

Fig. 100. After firing shots that stop an attack, lower the gun (l.) and scan first to one side (c.) then the other (r.). Shift your eyes only; don't turn your head or lose sight of the attacker.

Once you have moved to cover, and without taking your eyes off your assailant, call the police. Tell the dispatcher you were attacked and fired in self-defense, and you are holding the attacker at gunpoint. The dispatcher will give you instructions to follow when the police arrive; you should generally obey these instructions precisely, unless they will clearly increase your risk of being injured. Tell the dispatcher if your situation does not allow you to obey his or her instructions.

Until the police arrive, wait in your covered position, continue to observe your attacker, and hold your gun in a ready position. Do not talk to your

assailant except to yell short, decisive commands as necessary to maintain control over him or her; don't engage in conversation, as this may distract you. Do not leave your covered position to search for other intruders, and do not abandon cover to flee the scene (as to a neighbor's house) unless you are absolutely certain you can do so in safety. Remember, your attacker's accomplice may be lurking elsewhere in the building or outside your house.

Fig. 101. After firing shots at an attacker, you should move to cover and reload your firearm. Note that the defender is keeping her eyes forward to keep her assailant in view while she reloads.

If others are with you behind cover, keep them there. Do not send them to summon help or to the presumed greater safety of another location. This may expose them to danger from an unseen accomplice.

It may be extremely difficult for you to remain behind cover and watch the assailant you shot lie in excruciating pain in a pool of blood. You must mentally prepare yourself for the situation in which a predatory criminal, who just a few moments earlier was intent upon hurting or killing you, is now writhing on the floor in pain, crying out and begging for assistance. For many, this will be the hardest part of a shooting situation. Decent people do not enjoy inflicting suffering, even on a criminal who violently attacked them, and may feel sympathy for an attacker in pain.

Regardless of these feelings, you must keep your distance from that assailant and remain behind cover until police arrive. Your attacker may be shamming, waiting for you to approach so that he or she may use a hidden weapon against you. Alternatively, your shots may have only temporarily incapacitated your assailant, and he may suddenly revive when you come close.

A critical consideration that is often given little thought is the need to maintain the integrity of the shooting scene. When the police arrive, they will commence an investigation that will involve, among other things, all the physical evidence at the scene—bloodstains, footprints,

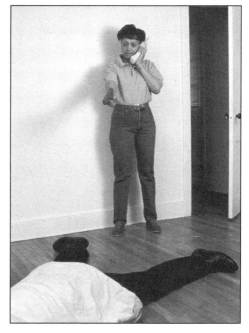

Fig. 102. If you are unable to safely move to cover after firing on an attacker, back up against a wall and use your non-dominant hand to call the police. Do not lose sight of your assailant.

shell casings, bullet holes and bullet fragments, and so on. It is absolutely essential that all physical evidence be undisturbed. Neither you nor any others at the shooting scene should move or touch anything.

Also, neighbors who hear the gunshots may come to look, help or investigate. Do not allow them to enter the shooting scene under any circumstances (unless, of course, one of your neighbors is a law enforcement officer). Intrusive neighbors may be exposing themselves to danger from your attacker or an undetected accomplice, may inadvertently or intentionally disturb evidence at the scene, and will, at the very least, cause confusion and make it more difficult for you—and later, the police—to control the situation. Anyone other than the police who arrives at the scene offering to "help" should be told to immediately leave the area and return home.

Sometimes an assailant you are forced to shoot will go down, seemingly incapacitated, then shortly revive. If the revived attacker again constitutes a threat—produces a weapon, for example, or continues to approach—you have no choice but to again use your defensive firearm.

On the other hand, if the aggressor recovers and flees the scene, do not attempt to stop or follow him. Let him go. It is not your job to capture criminals; in fact, there may be legal ramifications to pursuing your attacker, particularly if you end up shooting him (see Part V: Firearms, Self-Defense and the Law). Apprehending criminals is the job of the police. Armed with your description of your assailant, and with the knowledge that he will have to seek medical care, the police will have little difficulty in apprehending him.

GREETING THE POLICE

After any incident in which shots are fired, the police will inevitably arrive to investigate, summoned by either you or your neighbors. It is far preferable for the call for law enforcement assistance to originate with you, for only you can relate what has actually happened. When calling the police, answer the dispatcher's questions calmly and succinctly. Avoid being excited; not only will your excitement increase the likelihood of garbled communication, but the police officers responding to the call understandably will be leery of dealing with a hysterical person with a gun. Do not volunteer any information about the incident other than what is required to answer the dispatcher's questions regarding your immediate safety. Be sure to describe yourself, your attacker and any other people in the the immediate area, so that the police will know who is who when they arrive. Also, notify the dispatcher if your attacker still seems capable of posing a threat.

Even if you believe that a neighbor has called the police, it is still advisable for you to do so as well. You will be able to give the responding officers additional information and thus minimize confusion and the potential for a tragic error resulting from mistaken identity. Also, the dispatcher will be able to coordinate between you and the officers, relaying to you their instructions.

If you are talking to the dispatcher when the police arrive, you will receive precise instructions to allow the officers to safely take charge of the situation. Follow any instructions exactly and immediately; even though you know you're not the aggressor, the police only see you as a man or woman with a gun and, therefore, potentially dangerous. Most difficult are situations in which you are holding a still-dangerous attacker at gunpoint. In these situations, it is essential to apprise the responding officers of the circumstances, so that there is continuity of control of the aggressor.

In some situations, however, you may not have an opportunity to call a dispatcher before police arrive. They don't know that you successfully defended yourself from a predatory criminal; all they know is that shots were fired at a particular location. When they arrive, they have to assume, for their own safety, that any person with a firearm is a threat. Thus, if you behave in a manner that seems aggressive, you may survive the criminal attack but still be mistaken for the aggressor by the responding officers—with tragic consequences.

Whether you have contacted the police dispatcher or not, you should follow certain rules when greeting the police to ensure both their safety and yours. First and foremost, never greet or turn toward a police officer with a gun in your hand. The officers won't know you are the victim; they'll just see the gun swinging toward them. Also, follow all instructions precisely and immediately. Don't argue, hesitate, stall or give advice. Police officers are trained to take control of situations; if you seem to resist them, they have no choice but to assume you are uncooperative. All your movements should be slow and precise, and your hands should be visible at all times. Keep in mind that the more cooperative and rational you appear to the police officers, the more likely they will be to see you as the innocent victim that you are.

Fig. 103. When you open your safe room door to the responding police officers, your firearm should be unloaded and on the bed–not in your hand.

CHAPTER 17

THE AFTERMATH OF A DEFENSIVE SHOOTING

Complete preparation for defensive firearm use involves more than practicing the shooting fundamentals, shooting positions, and visualization exercises. True, when you are confronted by an assailant, your first concern is prevailing in the encounter, and the shooting skills you have learned are of paramount importance. When the shooting is over, however, you may experience emotional turmoil, social ostracism and even legal sanctions. These are all common aspects of the aftermath of a defensive shooting, and require prior mental preparation just as effective shooting and gun handling require physical preparation.

An important part of this mental preparation—indeed, a step that should be taken before you even decide to incorporate a firearm into your defense strategy—is to ensure that defensive firearm use is in accord with your own values. Ask yourself the following questions:

- *Am I prepared to take the life of another human being to save my own life or that of a loved one?*
- *Does my religion permit the taking of a life in self-defense?*
- *Do my personal moral standards permit the taking of a life in self-defense?*
- *Am I prepared to tolerate the judgement of my family, friends, and neighbors if I must defend myself with lethal force?*

Even when you are justified and forced to do so, shooting a predatory criminal is not a pleasant experience. Realize this and plan for it in your mental training.

EMOTIONAL AFTERMATH OF A DEFENSIVE SHOOTING

After prevailing in a violent encounter, you may experience a number of emotions. These emotions often occur in the order listed below, but are not universal; some people may not exhibit any of them, while others will experience some or all of the following emotional reactions, but in varying sequences.

Elation. Often there is an immediate feeling of elation at having survived and prevailed in a life-threatening encounter. In today's social and political atmosphere, attack survivors may feel that they should downplay or ignore this emotion. The survivor who feels this elation is not cold-bloodedly rejoicing at the death of another, however. Rather, it is a euphoria resulting from both a sense of relief at having survived, and an involuntary biochemical reaction resulting from the release of endorphins and other sensory- and mood-enhancing chemicals into the bloodstream. The feeling experienced by the victor in a defensive shooting is similar to—and just as uncontrollable as—the rush felt by a skydiver when the parachute opens. It is important to realize that there is nothing wrong with a momentary or lasting feeling of elation at having prevailed. Often this emotion is quickly followed by guilt at having felt elation in the first place.

Revulsion. After the initial elation at having survived the violent confrontation, there often arises a feeling of revulsion at what has happened. The victorious victim may become nauseous, vomit, or even faint from the emotional shock of seeing the result of the confrontation.

The absence of revulsion does not mean you are a bad or cold person. Your own experiences (such as military combat duty or work as an emergency medical technician) may have given you a greater tolerance for the unpleasant consequences of a shooting. However, in preparing for the aftermath of defensive firearm use, you must recognize that the scene of a shooting contains many distasteful and even sickening sights and sounds. While you cannot completely steel yourself to what you will see and hear, visualizing potential outcomes may decrease the distress you experience after a shooting.

Remorse. Many survivors experience remorse at having killed an attacker. This has nothing to do with the moral justifiability of their actions. It is simply a normal feeling of sadness or sorrow at having been forced to kill.

Self-Doubt. Those who prevail in a defensive shooting scenario may begin to replay the sequence of events in their minds, and ask themselves questions such as: Did I really have to shoot? Could I have avoided the attack? Was there something else I could have done? Like remorse, this feeling is a natural result of the normal person's aversion to taking a life, even when morally and legally justifiable.

Acceptance. This is usually the last of the emotional stages encountered after a defensive shooting. Rationalization is the first step to acceptance, and is often a consequence of the self-doubt described above. As you analyze the circumstances of the shooting, you will conclude that your actions were both justified and necessary.

There is no certainty that you will go through all or any of these emotional stages; nor can you be sure that you will arrive at the acceptance stage. Human emotions are much too complex to encase them in neat psychological boxes, or to arrange them in a simple sequence. Many shooting survivors, in fact, experience residual feelings of remorse and self-doubt, as well as other emotions, such as anger and fear.

As with other traumatic life experiences, you must put a defensive shooting in its proper place and move on. With time, the negative emotions associated with the event usually fade, allowing you to get on with your normal life. Don't dwell on the event, but also do not suppress your feelings about what has occurred. Most mental health experts agree that accepting and expressing your emotions is the first step in dealing with them.

Post-Traumatic Stress Disorder (PTSD). This term has been loosely (and often inappropriately) used in the popular media to describe a wide variety of reactions to stressful life events. Some (but not all) of the symptoms of PTSD include flashbacks, recurrent nightmares, and an inability to function normally (as to hold a job or maintain a stable marriage). Not everyone who has such experiences necessarily has PTSD; that diagnosis can be made only by a trained mental health worker. Nor is it true that everyone who goes through a traumatic event is inevitably afflicted with PTSD. Most people, in fact, who suffer extreme stress—airplane crash survivors, combat veterans, victims of tornadoes and other natural disasters, and the like—do not develop clinical PTSD.

REDUCING THE EMOTIONAL AFTERMATH OF A DEFENSIVE SHOOTING

Although you cannot avoid experiencing certain emotions as the result of your justifiable use of deadly force, you can prevent those emotions from taking control of your life. Two methods that many have found helpful are counseling and self-reinforcement.

Counseling. Counseling is one of the most effective and widely used ways that human beings have of working out their problems. Although the term may immediately bring to mind formal sessions with a psychotherapist, social worker or clergyman, in actuality counseling goes on everyday in our normal lives. Every time you unburden yourself to another—whether husband or wife, close friend, neighbor, or co-worker—a kind of informal counseling is going on.

Counseling achieves results in several ways. For one who has used deadly force to survive a deadly attack, talking to another sympathetic person about the experience gives the survivor support and affirmation, as well as the viewpoint of a detached third party. This objective viewpoint can be important in helping a survivor deal with overwhelming self-doubt and remorse, and in finally arriving at an acceptance of his or her actions.

Seeking counseling—whether with a professional or a friend or relative—should never be viewed as a sign of weakness. The survivor who obtains counseling is simply acknowledging two basic human truths: that two heads are often better than one, and that one may sometimes be unable to see the forest for the trees. A gun owner who is involved in a self-defense shooting may be too close to the event, emotionally and otherwise, to be able to step back and look at what transpired in a calm, rational, evenhanded manner—as could a friend, pastor or psychotherapist. It is no more a sign of weakness for the survivor of an attack to seek counseling than it is for a physician to get a colleague's advice on a particular surgical procedure. In both cases, counseling provides a fresh and objective point of view that may lead to greater understanding.

Counseling may be obtained from a variety of sources, including:
• psychiatrists, psychologists and other mental health professionals;
• clergy;
• your spouse;
• trusted friends; and
• others who have had similar experiences.

Many police forces have counselors for officers involved in shootings. Such law enforcement agencies may be able to refer you to appropriate counseling resources.

Following any defensive shooting encounter, however, the first type of counseling you should seek is legal counseling. Consult with your attorney before speaking to others about the incident.

Self-Reinforcement. Self-reinforcement is a technique by which you replace negative, self-destructive thoughts with positive, self-affirming ones. In a sense, you are acting as your own counselor, giving yourself support and validating the actions you took in self-defense.

Self-reinforcement can and should be practiced by anyone who has had to defend himself or herself with deadly force. Self-reinforcing statements should take the following form:
• *I am a good person.*
• *I did not choose to attack another law-abiding citizen.*
• *I did not attack anyone. I was attacked by a criminal.*
• *I did not invade the sanctity of another's home.*
• *My attacker was the one who chose a lifestyle and sequence of events that led to his injury or death.*
• *I was morally justified in protecting my life with deadly force.*
• *I have quite possibly saved the lives of others by stopping this preda-*

tor from harming future innocent victims.
• *I had no choice but to use deadly force to stop my attacker.*
• *I am a moral person.*

It may be useful to write or type these self-reinforcements on a piece of paper you can carry in your wallet or purse, so you can bolster yourself whenever assailed by self-doubt. Ultimately, you are the only person who can make it possible for you to put a defensive shooting into proper perspective and get on with your life.

LEGAL AFTERMATH OF A DEFENSIVE SHOOTING

The legal ramifications of being involved in a self-defense shooting vary depending upon the laws applicable in your jurisdiction. In many areas, both the police and the prosecutor's office have some discretion in the way in which a defensive shooting is handled. If you are involved in an absolutely clearcut case of self-defense, you may only have to answer questions at the police station and make a formal statement. However, if the circumstances around the shooting incident are initially unclear, you could be arrested. In a worst-case scenario, it is possible that you could be charged with a felony, arrested and taken out of your home in handcuffs; taken to a police station and fingerprinted, photographed, booked and put into a cell; and held in jail until the charges against you are dropped or bail is arranged. Furthermore, your defensive handgun, and probably any other firearms in your home, could be confiscated by the police. Additionally, you will undoubtedly incur hefty legal bills in your own defense.

A more complete discussion of the legal issues revolving around the self-defense use of a firearm is found in Part V: Firearms, Self-Defense and the Law. The defense-oriented gun owner is strongly encouraged to consult a qualified attorney familiar with the gun laws and self-defense laws of the gun owner's jurisdiction.

SOCIAL AFTERMATH OF A DEFENSIVE SHOOTING

In addition to the emotional and legal aftermath that follows the use of a firearm in self-defense, there are social consequences as well. Your neighbors may hear the gunshots you fired to save your life; in any event they will certainly observe the police cars that will arrive at your house. They could see you taken away in handcuffs, or your assailant carried off on a stretcher or in a

Fig. 104. Even if your use of a firearm in self-defense was legitimate, you might still have to suffer the embarassment and stress of being arrested.

body bag. Even if you are eventually fully exonerated, some will still see you as "that trigger-happy nut" or some other unflattering designation. You will be the target of those who hate guns and distrust gun owners, as well as those who can't stand the thought of anyone acting in self-defense. Some of your co-workers and neighbors will begin to act differently toward you, avoiding you, shunning you or treating you with outright hostility. Your self-defense act may impact negatively on your job advancement if your superiors don't like, or are afraid of, guns. You may get anonymous threatening notes at work, or crank calls at home from people who cannot accept what you've done. People may stare at you in stores, and you may find yourself unexpectedly challenged by those who identify with, or were friends with, your assailant.

Worst of all may be the effects on your family. Your spouse may find himself or herself socially ostracized, and your children may have to endure cruel taunts from their classmates at school—or even critical comments from their teachers. You may even have members of your own family who cannot understand what you had to do. And if you have small children, you will have the difficult task of explaining to them why you were taken away in handcuffs by the police.

There can be substantial unforeseen consequences when you are forced to use your firearm for self-defense. Your ordeal will not end merely when the attack is stopped; the emotional, legal and social aftermath probably will continue for weeks, months or even years after the event. This aftermath is one more reason why the seriousness of the responsibility of owning a firearm for self defense cannot be overly emphasized.

PART V:
FIREARMS, SELF-DEFENSE AND THE LAW

CHAPTER 18

FIREARMS, SELF-DEFENSE AND THE LAW

We live in a society of laws—laws that impact on most areas of our lives. Gun ownership is one of the most heavily regulated of those areas. It is critical for the defensive gun owner to have at least a basic working knowledge of the local, state, and federal laws that govern the purchase, possession, transportation and transfer of firearms, as well as their use in defensive situations. Also essential is an understanding of the basic legal principles surrounding the use of deadly force in self-defense.

LEGAL REQUIREMENTS GOVERNING THE PURCHASE AND OWNERSHIP OF HANDGUNS

Nationwide, there are more than 20,000 federal, state and local laws regulating gun purchase and ownership. Many of these apply specifically to handguns. Outlined below are some of the provisions of the major gun laws currently in effect.

Gun Control Act of 1968. This law, passed partially in response to the tragic assassinations of Martin Luther King, Jr. and Robert F. Kennedy, Jr., eliminated the mail order purchase of modern firearms (those made after 1898) and established a variety of classes of persons prohibited from owning or possessing a firearm. These prohibited persons include felons, those who use illegal drugs, those who have been committed to a mental institution, those who are not U.S. citizens and those who have renounced their U.S. citizenship.

Bureau of Alcohol, Tobacco and Firearms (BATF) Form 4473. All persons purchasing a firearm—whether it is a rifle, shotgun or handgun—from a federally licensed gun dealer must complete a BATF Form 4473. This form contains information on the buyer, the serial number and description of the firearm or firearms purchased, and the name and address of the Federal Firearms License holder. Additionally, the Form 4473 has a section in which the prospective purchaser attests to whether he or she falls into any of the classes of persons prohibited from owning a firearm. Giving a false answer to any item on Form 4473 is a felony punishable by a fine or imprisonment.

Brady Law. This 1994 law was named for gun-control advocates James and Sarah Brady, who were instrumental in its adoption. In its initial form the law mandated a number of provisions for gun buyers, several of which have since expired. As of this writing, the Brady Law now requires a national computerized instant background check of all persons purchasing a firearm from a Federal Firearms License holder.

Violent Crime Control and Law Enforcement Act. This law, also known as the **1994 Crime Bill,** prohibits the sale, transfer or possession of magazines for semi-automatic firearms having a capacity of more than 10 rounds. The law also contained a list of banned semi-automatic firearms (erroneously labeled as "assault weapons"), and established certain combinations of features (including, among others, pistol grips, flash suppressors and folding stocks) that may also make other firearms fall into the "assault weapon" category.

With the expiration of the 1994 Crime Bill in 2005, the above mentioned federal prohibitions against "assault weapons" and high-capacity magazines are no longer in effect. Nonetheless, some of the Crime Bill's provisions have been incorporated into the laws of several states, but there are still many other federal laws in effect such as those that govern the ability of semi-automatic firearms from imported parts.

Lautenburg Amendment. This law, named for New Jersey Senator Ed Lautenburg, expands the list of persons prohibited from possessing firearms or ammunition to include anyone who has been found guilty of a misdemeanor crime of domestic violence. The prohibition also applies to persons under certain restraining orders. This far-reaching law is retroactive—that is, anyone who has ever been found guilty of, or who has pleaded guilty to such a crime, is subject to firearm forfeiture. The law also makes it a felony for anyone in the prohibited category to possess any firearms or ammunition.

State and Local Laws. In addition to federal laws, further restrictions are imposed by numerous state and local laws. For example, in some states a permit to purchase must first be obtained before a firearm can be bought. Successful completion of the permit process may result in the issuance of a gun owner identification card.

Many states and municipalities also have enacted laws that prohibit or restrict certain classes of firearms based on type (such as semi-automatic pistols or so-called Saturday Night Specials), magazine capacity or other characteristics, sometimes resulting in a list of state-approved guns. Waiting periods and background checks prior to purchase, and registration of guns owned, are also required by law in some jurisdictions. And, of course, there are almost always fees accompanying the permits, background checks and registration applications. Specific legal requirements will vary for each different state, and also may vary among the counties and municipalities within a state.

Intrastate and Interstate Acquisition and Transfer. Generally speaking, there are two ways to acquire a firearm: from a federally licensed dealer, or from a private individual. Federally licensed dealers include gun shops, professional gunsmiths, and other businesses, such as hardware stores and pawn shops. Whenever you purchase a firearm through a federally-licensed dealer, you must meet the requirements of BATF Form 4473, plus any additional restrictions imposed by state or local law.

In many states, the transfer of a firearm by a resident of that state to a resident of that state—whether as the result of sale, gift, loan, or bequest—is considered a simple property transaction between two private individuals, and need not go through a federally licensed dealer. In other states, some or all firearms transfers between individuals must go through a federally licensed dealer. Note that even in those states in which transfers between private citizens do not go through FFL holders, the seller still may not transfer a gun to an individual falling into any of the classes of persons prohibited by law from possessing a firearm.

Note also that, for legal purposes, transfer does not necessarily mean selling. Anytime you allow a person to possess one of your firearms—that is, have it under their physical or constructive control—you have, for that period of time, transferred the firearm to that person. Thus, depending upon your state's laws, allowing a person in a prohibited class to simply hold one of your guns in his or her hands (whether the gun is loaded or not) may constitute a transfer of possession, and thus may be illegal.

Interstate transfers of handguns always must go through federally licensed gun dealers, whether the transfer is between an individual and a gun shop, or between two individuals, in different states. If the transfer is between two individuals, the one transferring the gun may send it directly to the FFL holder in the recipient's state of residence, who will transfer it to the recipient. Alternatively, the person transferring the handgun may take it to an FFL holder in his or her state of residence, who will arrange to ship the gun to the FFL holder in the recipient's state of residence. In either case, the recipient will have to observe all the legal requirements, such as Form 4473 and Brady Law instant check provisions, that apply to a handgun sale.

Various jurisdictions may have additional laws regarding firearms sales and non-sale firearms transfers, such as gifts or bequests, as well as transfers to certain classes of people, such as minors.

Handgun Possession and Transportation. Legally, *possession* is defined as the holding or occupancy of a thing such that physical control can be exerted over it. Legal ownership, or title, is not a requirement for possession. Many different federal, state and local laws relate to handgun possession under various circumstances.

At the present time, federal law imposes few if any restrictions on possession in one's home, business or vehicle, or in public places. However, federal law does prohibit possession of a firearm in federal government offices or buildings, such as post offices, IRS offices and the like. Possession may also be prohibited or restricted in other areas, including (but not limited to) military bases, some federal lands (such as national parks), and school zones. Note that a state or local carry permit does not nullify federal restrictions on gun possession on federal property.

Virtually all states and local jurisdictions have laws regulating handgun possession. The restrictions imposed by these laws vary considerably from jurisdiction to jurisdiction, and situation from situation. Your rights and obligations likely will vary depending upon whether you possess the firearm in your home, a temporary residence (such as a hotel or campground), or a vehicle. Even in your home or business, your specific rights may be contingent upon whether you are physically inside the structure, or outside on your own lawn or grounds. Moreover, your rights regarding possession on your person in public places will vary. Some states allow you to carry your handgun openly, without a permit; many others have a permit process if you wish to carry a concealed handgun, and other jurisdictions permit you to have your firearm on your person only if it is unloaded and locked in a case.

Many states, counties and municipalities also have laws prohibiting the possession of firearms in schools or government offices or buildings, similar to the federal laws previously mentioned.

Transporting a handgun within a jurisdiction is generally subject to that jurisdiction's laws regarding possession in public. If you

Fig. 105. In many jurisdictions, a firearm must be transported in a locked case in an inaccessible part of the vehicle.

The Basics of Personal Protection in the Home

hold a state concealed-carry permit, for example, you can usually carry a firearm in the passenger compartment of a vehicle without having to lock it up or otherwise make it inaccessible. Some states have specific laws regarding the transportation of hunting firearms to and from a game area. In other jurisdictions, you may legally transport your firearm in your vehicle only if it is unloaded, locked in a case and secured in a locked trunk or other inaccessible part of your vehicle, with ammunition in a separate inaccessible locked container. This is also the recommended method for carrying firearms in your vehicle on interstate (federal) highways.

Some states and other jurisdictions require the registration of any firearm located within their boundaries, even temporarily, or totally prohibit the possession of certain types of guns. The **1986 McClure-Volkmer Gun Owner's Protection Act** exempts firearm owners who are transporting their arms interstate from the laws of such jurisdictions (as long as the gun owner is merely passing through the jurisdiction). The firearm should be locked in an inaccessible part of the vehicle as described above. Although the federal Gun Owner's Protection Act overrides state and local law, in practice a gun owner may still be harassed or arrested by overzealous local law enforcement officials who don't know about the federal law.

Transporting a firearm on public transportation—a bus, train, subway or aircraft—is regulated both by applicable local, state and federal law, as well as any specific requirements of the transportation company or authority. If you are transporting the firearm within the boundaries of a state and have a state-issued concealed carry permit, you may be able to carry your gun on any mode of public transportation. The most notable exception to this is an airline flight. Only sky marshals and certain other types of law enforcement or security officers are allowed to carry firearms on their persons aboard commercial aircraft.

When transporting a firearm across state lines via public transportation, the firearm usually must be unloaded and locked in an approved case, and you must give the carrier written notice that a firearm or ammunition is being transported. This is also the procedure for transporting a firearm aboard any commercial airline. Other restrictions and procedures (such as a special check-in procedure) may also apply.

THE USE OF DEADLY FORCE IN SELF-DEFENSE

There are many legal definitions, theories and principles surrounding the use of deadly force for self-protection. It is beyond the scope of this chapter to discuss these in detail; only a brief outline of the major concepts can be presented. *You are strongly advised to consult an attorney for a more thorough explanation of your rights and responsibilities in relation to armed self-defense in your jurisdiction.*

The "Reasonable Man" Standard. In judging the legality of a person's conduct, it is often necessary to determine whether a party acted in a way that was appropriate or reasonable. This determination is often made by judging whether a hypothetical "reasonable man" would act in a similar way under the same conditions. By such a "reasonable man" standard, for example, shooting an intruder who approached you with a weapon despite your verbal warnings likely would be deemed justifiable, because the reasonable man would consider the intruder's actions to be immediately life-threatening. Shooting an unarmed intruder who is 50 feet away and who does not approach you might not be considered justifiable, because a reasonable man would not necessarily consider such a person a threat requiring the use of deadly force.

Be aware that a judge or jury, in applying the "reasonable man"

Fig. 106. The Reasonable Force doctrine may, in some cases, allow an innocent victim of an attack to use deadly force against an unarmed person, as when the unarmed attacker is much bigger or stronger than the intended victim.

standard to an action, is making a judgment about a chain of events that occurred under stress and over the course of a few seconds or less. What may seem reasonable to you or to most people under the conditions of an immediate violent attack might be unreasonable to a jury sitting in the comfort and safety of a courtroom.

Use of Reasonable Force. The degree or amount of force you can use in defending yourself must be reasonable—that is, proportional to the level of threat presented. In rough terms, you can't use a gun to defend yourself from a slap in the face. A 300-pound, 30-year-old professional football player attacked by an unarmed 135-pound, 70-year-old man would not be justified in using deadly force to defend himself, due to the relatively low level of threat the smaller, older man represented to him. On the other hand, if the 70-year-old attacker was armed with a knife or gun, the football player might then be justified in using deadly force to defend himself (if certain other conditions are also met).

By law, you can sometimes use force in a number of circumstances—to protect your property from theft or vandalism, for example, or to remove a trespasser from your property. The amount of force you are legally allowed to use, however, must be only that amount required to effect the desired result—only that force needed to keep an angry neighbor from smashing up your car with a baseball bat, for example, and no more. Deadly force is not legally justified in such situations.

Use of Deadly Force. The justifiable use of deadly force is limited only to situations in which certain requirements are met. Although those requirements may vary somewhat in different jurisdictions, there are some fairly universal guidelines. Deadly force can only be used by an innocent victim of an attack, and only when that attack represents a threat of serious bodily harm or death; it cannot be used to defend property rights. This threat of serious bodily harm or death must be imminent (about to happen immediately) and within the ability of the attacker. *In addition, in some situations, the victim of an attacker must first retreat (or attempt to do so if safely possible) before being able to utilize deadly force in self-defense.*

Ability of an Attacker. An attacker is considered to represent a threat to life or limb only if they are actually capable of causing death or serious injury. In the sample situation presented earlier, a small, elderly, unarmed man generally would not be considered to have the ability to threaten the life or limb of a large, young, muscular man. Even if the elderly man demonstrated the intent to kill the younger man (as by screaming, "I'll kill you!"), deadly force would generally not be justified in repelling his attack, as the hypothetical "reasonable man" would not consider him capable of following through on that intent.

Fig. 107. Persons making threats at a distance are not considered by the Reasonable Man standard to be an imminent threat. The use of deadly force against such persons would therefore not be justified.

Presence of an Imminent Threat. Another requirement for the use of deadly defensive force is that the threat of death or serious bodily harm must be imminent—that is, about to occur immediately. A future threat to your life and limb does not generally justify the present use of deadly force. For example, if a predator threatens, "Someday soon I'm going to catch you alone and blow you away," you cannot respond by immediately using deadly force against him— even if he is, say, a paroled murderer whom you know is fully capable of making good on his threat. You will be legally able to defend yourself with a deadly weapon only at the point that his threat becomes real and imminent.

Innocent Victim of Attack. For you to claim justifiable self-defense in your use of deadly force, you must not yourself have caused or incited your assailant's attack. For example, you cannot provoke a person into attacking you and then shoot him or her in self-defense. Nor can you respond to an attacker in a way that further incites or inflames him or her. For example, if you were to innocently step on another person's shoes, he might react by shoving you. You are not entitled to escalate the situation to the level of deadly force by using

your firearm.

Duty to Retreat. In many self-defense situations, you have a duty to retreat from a confrontation before you can legally use deadly force to defend yourself. Duty to retreat simply means that you must attempt to physically escape or evade a confrontation if you can do so safely. You are not obligated to retreat if doing so will expose you to greater danger.

Most states require you to retreat from confrontations occurring in public. In many jurisdictions, however, you may not be obligated to retreat from an attacker in your own home or on your own property. Consult an attorney for the laws applicable in your area.

Brandishing. In many if not most jurisdictions, brandishing, or displaying your firearm in a threatening or aggressive manner, is illegal

Fig. 108. Brandishing a firearm is illegal in most jurisdictions, and may undermine any subsequent claim of legitimate self-defense.

and may undermine your claim of legitimate self-defense. As a practical matter, if you brandish your firearm to deter an attacker, it may be unclear to both witnesses and law enforcement authorities exactly who is the aggressor and who is the victim.

Castle Doctrine. This doctrine, derived from English common law and expressed in the familiar saying, "A man's home is his castle," gives you special rights in your own home that you may enjoy nowhere else. For example, in many jurisdictions you have no duty to retreat from an attacker in your own home. Also, in some jurisdictions, the very presence of an intruder in your home may allow you to treat him as a threat. Some jurisdictions also allow you to extend the Castle Doctrine beyond your home to include any place you might be domiciled for the night, such as a friend's house, hotel room, campground and so on. Other rights may also derive from the Castle Doctrine, depending upon the laws in your jurisdiction.

Fig 109. In virtually every jurisdiction, you must cease using deadly force when your attacker is no longer a threat.

Cessation of Threat. You are entitled to use deadly force against an attacker only as long as they present a threat. Once the threat has ceased— as by their flight, surrender, or inability to continue the attack—so must your use of lethal force.

SUMMARY

The above material is merely a partial overview of some of the many complex legal issues concerning firearm ownership, firearm use, and the employment of deadly force in self-defense. Every gun owner should seek additional information from an attorney familiar with the firearm and self-defense laws in his or her jurisdiction.

CHAPTER 19

THE LEGAL AFTERMATH OF A SHOOTING

NOTE: This chapter is not intended to take the place of consultation with a qualified attorney, nor should it be construed as providing general or specific legal advice. The information contained herein is intended to provide broad general guidelines regarding the legal ramifications that might stem from a self-defense shooting in some jurisdictions. For more specific information, consult an attorney familiar with the laws relating to firearms and self-defense in your jurisdiction.

Whether it involves the acquisition and mastery of shooting skills or the development of a defensive mindset, preparedness is the key to prevailing in a violent attack. Preparedness of a different type is also essential to survive the potential legal aftermath of a defensive shooting. The prudent gun owner must become thoroughly familiar with the potential legal ramifications of defensive gun use in his or her jurisdiction.

It is important for the defense-oriented gun owner to secure legal representation before he or she is involved in a shooting situation. Selecting a lawyer out of the telephone book at the police station is not likely to provide you with the kind of representation you will need. Any attorney you select should be thoroughly familiar with all applicable federal, state and local laws regarding firearm ownership and self-defense. The attorney should also be apprised of any particulars of your own situation that would be relevant to any police investigation that would follow defensive firearm use.

Contact your state bar association for a list of attorneys in your area, along with their specialties. Members of your gun club may be able to recommend attorneys with experience in Second Amendment and self-defense cases. Also, firearm-friendly attorneys may post their cards at gun shops or on gun club bulletin boards. As a service to its members, the NRA also offers a referral service that matches attorneys with those needing legal representation.

The following describes some of the possible legal outcomes that may be faced by a survivor of a self-defense shooting.

ARREST

In all jurisdictions, a shooting that results in injury or death will entail an investigation. It may be sufficiently clear from the circumstances of the

Fig. 110. You may be arrested if you injure or kill a violent assailant in self-defense. Such an arrest would be both embarrassing and traumatic to you and your family.

incident that your actions were completely in legitimate self-defense; in such cases, depending upon the discretion allowed the police and prosecutor's office, you may only have to face the inconvenience of a police questioning. Under other circumstances—for example, if you knew and had previously quarreled with the person you shot—the police and prosecutor may consider your actions to be illegal. In such circumstances, you likely will be arrested, booked, fingerprinted and photographed. You will be put into a cell and held until the charges against you are dropped, or your bail is secured by your attorney. Either way, you will spend at least a few hours in jail, and possibly several days.

FIFTH & SIXTH AMENDMENT PROTECTIONS

The Fifth Amendment of the United States Constitution provides you with certain rights and protections, chief among them being that you have no obligation to talk to the police until you have consulted with your attorney. The Sixth Amendment gives you the right to have your attorney present during all questioning.

When the police arrive, you can refuse to answer their questions until your attorney is present. Of course, you should exercise some common sense in this; you may not need a lawyer to respond to such questions as "Where's the bathroom?" Also, you may want to provide police with information that they need to ensure the immediate safety of the area, such as "Which way did the assailant flee?" However, most attorneys advise that you politely but firmly refuse to discuss the shooting incident until you have consulted with legal counsel. Under the stress and emotions that follow involvement in a life-threatening situation, you may not think or communicate clearly, and may utter something that could be used against you in a subsequent legal proceeding.

Even before you become involved in a defensive shooting, it is highly advisable to discuss with your attorney exactly what you may and may not say to police should you have to use a firearm in self-defense. Just as you prepare mentally and physically to survive a violent encounter, this legal preparation may help you better negotiate the criminal justice system.

GUN CONFISCATION

If you are arrested by the police, they may also take your defensive firearm and, sometimes, any other firearms in your home. After all, from their point of view, you may be a suspect in a felony—assault with a deadly weapon or, if your attacker dies, homicide. The problem often lies in getting them back. In some areas—particularly those in which officials are hostile to Second Amendment rights—you may have to go to court to secure the return of your guns.

Furthermore, police departments usually mark items taken as evidence. If you are lucky, they may put their mark—a number or letters scratched or stamped into the metal—in an unobtrusive location. Also, the police may or may not treat your guns with the same care as you would. In a "worst-case" situation, you may receive your guns back with dings and scratches from careless handling, evidence marks on external surfaces, and bore corrosion from having been fired and not cleaned. (If a department suspects that any of your firearms may have been used in a crime, technicians may fire them to obtain reference bullet specimens.)

SEARCH OF YOUR HOME

A full discussion of the rules governing permissible police searches is well beyond the scope of this text. Generally, to conduct a search in your home, police need a warrant for that location specifying what is being sought. There are several exceptions to this requirement, however; consult your attorney for more information.

Any normal law-abiding person may have objects, records, and so forth that are not at all illegal, but may be of a sensitive, private or even embarrassing nature. Such objects may become public knowledge as a result of a search. Of perhaps greater concern, during a search the police will almost certainly observe and make note of (mentally, at least) any books, magazines or other items that may cast doubt on the justifiability of your defensive shooting. For example, the fact that you possess material relating to sniping techniques or paramilitary operations may work against you in a court of law should you face criminal or civil charges as the result of your defensive gun use. The fact that you are simply a military history buff will likely not counter the perception among some of the jury that you are a bloodthirsty, trigger-happy gun owner looking for an opportunity to apply the killing techniques you enjoy reading about. Similarly, inflammatory signs in your home or office, such as "Protected by .38 Special" or "If I Find You Here Tonight, They'll Find You Here Tomorrow Morning" may also serve to undermine your claim of justifiable self-defense.

CRIME SCENE RESTRICTIONS

The area in which a shooting—even a justifiable one— takes place may be treated by police as a crime scene. This area could be immediately roped off and access granted only to police officers or crime scene technicians. While evidence is being gathered you might not be allowed to enter or cross the area, even if it is your own bedroom or office. In the meantime you may have to put up with a seemingly endless parade of evidence collectors, photographers, and other investigators in your home or business. In a cut-and-dried, clearcut case of self-defense, you may be inconvenienced for only an hour or so, but be forewarned that crime scenes sometimes are restricted for days or weeks until the forensic investigations are completed.

SUSPENSION OF GUN OWNERSHIP OR CARRY PERMITS

If you have a carry permit from your state, or if your state requires a permit merely to own a firearm, you should anticipate that it will likely be suspended or revoked following your arrest for shooting your assailant, particularly if the criminal charges against you are not dropped but are pursued by prosecutors. You may have to reapply for that permit once you are cleared of all criminal charges.

CRIMINAL TRIAL

In some cases, the criminal charges against you may be pursued instead of dropped. This may occur whenever the police or the prosecutor has questions regarding your claim of legitimate self-defense. This might be the case, for example, if you had had a previous disagreement with the assailant you shot, or if the witness testimony or physical evidence is contradictory or ambiguous.

Various areas of the country differ in their support of the right of armed self-defense. In some large cities, for example, in which both citizens and public officials have little sympathy for Second Amendment rights, you may be more likely to be put on trial for using a firearm to protect yourself than in rural areas or small towns.

CIVIL SUIT

Even if you are cleared of all criminal charges, you still may have to face a civil suit brought by your assailant or the assailant's family or estate. There are differences between a criminal and civil trial. Criminal charges can only be brought by the government, and can result in incarceration, fines, property seizure and certain other sanctions. A civil suit can be brought by anyone, and results only in the awarding of money or other non-incarceration relief, such as an order restricting your interaction with the plaintiff. Another important difference between a criminal and civil suit lies in the standard used to determine the outcome of a trial. In a criminal case, the jury (or judge) must be convinced by the evidence beyond a reasonable doubt. In a civil case, however, judgment is made for the plaintiff or defendant based upon a preponderance of the evidence. The standard is much higher in a criminal case than a civil case because the potential sanctions of a criminal conviction, such as lengthy incarceration or even the death penalty, are much more severe than the mere money award that is typical in a civil case.

If you use your firearm in self-defense and are later tried and found not guilty of any criminal charge, you should understand that such a verdict does not preclude a civil proceeding against you. Regardless of the outcome of a criminal trial, you may be subject to liability in a civil action.

LEGAL FEES

Even in the best of outcomes, in which no criminal charges against you are pressed and no civil suit is filed, you will usually still owe your attorney at least several hundred dollars, just to represent you at a bail hearing or during police interrogation. If you are forced to defend yourself against criminal charges in a full-scale trial—or if the assailant or the assailant's family sue you in civil court—your legal bills will amount to thousands, quite possibly tens of thousands of dollars.

SUMMARY

As can be seen from the above, even when an armed citizen prevails in a violent confrontation, he or she will still have to endure the vagaries of the criminal justice system. It is not enough to prepare yourself only to thwart an attack; you must also be ready for the legal aftermath that is sure to follow your use of deadly force.

PART VI:
SELECTING FIREARMS, AMMUNITION AND ACCESSORIES FOR PERSONAL PROTECTION

CHAPTER 20

SELECTING A FIREARM FOR PERSONAL PROTECTION

Choosing to own a handgun for personal protection requires careful consideration of a number of factors. The selection of a specific firearm and ammunition for self-defense can be just as critical, and should entail the same comprehensive deliberation.

A firearm is a tool for delivering energy at a distance. This energy can be used to do various tasks—to harvest game, punch a hole through a paper target, or, in the case of a defensive arm, stop a criminal attack.

GUN FIT

★ One of the most important factors contributing to a shooter's ability to shoot quickly and accurately is gun fit. *Gun fit* refers to how comfortably and naturally the firearm fits the hand—how well the firearm's grip size, grip angle, location of controls, length, size and other characteristics fit a particular shooter. Related to gun fit is *gun ergonomics*, a term that relates to the convenience and efficiency of the positioning of controls and gripping surfaces. Gun fit is highly individual: for example, guns that are suited for those with large, fleshy hands may not fit those having small, bony hands, and vice versa.

Good gun fit allows you to

Fig. 111. Good gun fit is critical to fast, accurate defensive shooting. Photos A and B show proper hand and trigger finger placement, made possible through proper gun fit, while C shows the gap between the trigger finger and frame that should exist when the gun fits the hand and fingers correctly.

183

maintain a consistent grip, positions your trigger finger in the proper location on the trigger, and facilitates your assumption of a stable shooting position. Before you purchase a gun, you should test-fire a number of different models to determine which fits you best. Guidance on gun fit can be provided by NRA Certified Instructors.

Test-firing a variety of handguns also will give you the opportunity to experience different action mechanisms. While there are a variety of handgun types, including single- and double-action revolvers, single-action, double-action and double-action-only semi-automatics, derringers and even single-shots, the novice defensive shooter will be best served by either a double-action revolver or a double-action semi-automatic.

REVOLVER OR SEMI-AUTOMATIC?

Among firearm instructors, gun writers and other authorities, both revolvers and semi-autos have their passionate adherents. Each type has strengths and limitations.

The *double-action revolver* often is recommended for new shooters because of its simplicity of operation and reliability. Once its cylinder is loaded, it is fired simply by pulling the trigger; no safety levers need be disengaged. Because the revolver does not depend upon the recoil generated by the cartridge for operation, it is capable of handling a wide variety of loadings in a particular

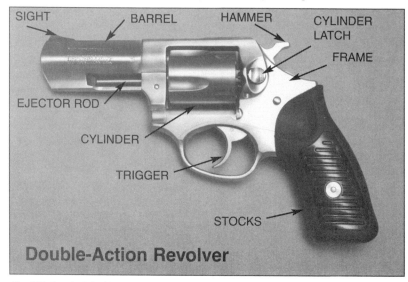

Fig. 112. A typical double-action revolver, showing some of the major features and components.

chambering. Moreover, the revolver's mechanism confers at least a theoretical reliability edge.

The main drawback to the revolver as a defensive arm is its limited ammunition capacity. Most defensive center-fire revolvers have a cylinder capacity of only 5 or 6 rounds—considerably less than the magazine capacity of most semi-automatic pistols.The revolver is also slow to reload, even with speedloaders (devices which allow the quick, simultaneous insertion of all the rounds into the cylinder). Additionally, each shot with the revolver must be fired using a long, relatively heavy trigger pull that some shooters find detrimental to accuracy.

The *semi-automatic pistol* (sometimes called a *self-loader*) has, in recent years, largely superseded the revolver as the handgun of choice for law enforcement officers and other armed professionals. Semi-autos have always had wide popularity among civilian shooters.

The popularity of semi-automatic arms stems from several factors. First, they generally have considerably greater cartridge capacity than revolvers of similar size, allowing more shots to be fired before reloading is necessary. When reloading is required, the semi-automatic can be reloaded with a full magazine much more quickly than a revolver's cylinder can be filled, even with speedloaders. Also, although the initial shot from a typical double-action semi-automatic is fired using a long and heavy trigger pull similar to that of a double-action revolver, each subsequent shot is fired by a short, light, single-action pull, which is generally considered to contribute to accuracy. (This advantage is

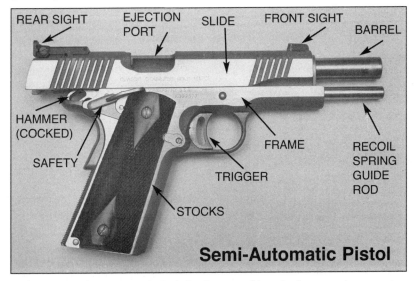

REAR SIGHT   EJECTION   SLIDE   FRONT SIGHT
              PORT   BARREL

HAMMER
(COCKED)
                                      FRAME   RECOIL
   SAFETY   SPRING
                           TRIGGER   GUIDE
                                               ROD

              STOCKS

Semi-Automatic Pistol

Fig. 113. A typical semi-automatic pistol, showing some of the major features and components.

negated on double-action-only semi-automatics, in which every shot is fired in double-action mode.) Lastly, the semi-auto generally is narrower in width than the revolver—a factor when concealment or cramped gun storage space is a concern.

Semi-automatics have several limitations, however. They are more ammunition-sensitive than revolvers, as they require cartridges within a certain power range to ensure that their recoil-operated mechanisms function properly. Also, their rapidly-moving parts make them somewhat more jam-prone than revolvers (although the reliability of today's semi-autos generally is excellent). Semi-automatic mechanisms usually include safety levers, decocking levers and/or slide release levers, making them initially less intuitive to operate. Furthermore, on virtually all semi-automatics, the slide must be manually retracted and released to chamber a round. The stiffness of the recoil springs on many semi-autos makes these pistols difficult to use by those with low hand and arm strength, arthritis or other physical limitations. Such individuals also may find it difficult to hold the semi-automatic pistol rigidly enough to ensure reliable operation.

CARTRIDGE SELECTION

For either type of firearm, there is a wide range of cartridges to choose from. The effectiveness of a self-defense firearm is related, to some extent, to the amount of energy it can deliver. This energy is usually expressed in terms of a measure called *kinetic energy* or *muzzle energy*, which is calculated using both bullet weight and bullet velocity, and is expressed in foot-pounds. Different cartridges are capable

Fig. 114. These photographs reflect the difference between a cartridge generating a low level of recoil and flash (above) and a cartridge producing considerable recoil and flash. Note the height of muzzle flip in the photo at right; this would make fast, accurate follow-up shots difficult to perform.

The Basics of Personal Protection in the Home

of generating different levels of kinetic energy, and thus vary in their ability to stop an assailant. Cartridge characteristics also influence the ability of the shooter to place shots precisely and rapidly on the target and to handle recoil.

As a general rule, you should select the most powerful cartridge that you can handle effectively—that is, one that does not produce flinching or excessive recoil, and allows you to apply follow-up shots quickly and accurately. This is determined primarily by test-firing handguns chambered for different cartridges. If possible, try handguns of different weights and sizes in the same chambering. If you find it difficult to handle the recoil generated by the .38 Special cartridge in a small, lightweight revolver, you might more easily control a heavier, bigger gun chambered for the same cartridge.

As a broad generalization, most firearm authorities recommend a minimum of 9 mm Parabellum (also known as 9 mm Para, 9 mm Luger, or 9x19 mm) for semi-automatic pistols, and .38 Special for revolvers. However, there are some shooters whose recoil sensitivity or lack of hand strength do not permit them to handle even these rather moderate-power cartridges. Such individuals should not feel themselves hopelessly undergunned with a pistol or revolver in .38 S&W, .380 Auto, .32 Auto, .25 Auto or even .22 Long Rifle. With proper bullet placement, even such low-powered rounds have proven effective for self-defense.

More detailed information on cartridge selection will be presented in Chapter 21: Selecting Ammunition for Personal Protection.

ADDITIONAL FACTORS

In addition to gun fit and chambering, other factors may influence handgun selection. *Gun size* is significant if the firearm may also be used for concealed carry purposes or if firearm storage space is minimal. *Safety features* are always of concern, particularly when the gun is used or stored in an environment in which there are children or other persons unauthorized to handle firearms. *Manufacturer's reputation* and *price* usually also play a part in any gun's purchase. An NRA Certified Instructor can assist the prospective gun owner in evaluating these factors.

CHAPTER 21

SELECTING AMMUNITION FOR PERSONAL PROTECTION

After the caliber, type of firearm, and specific firearm model are selected, the defensive-oriented shooter must still choose a particular load (a specific combination of bullet weight, bullet design, and muzzle velocity) among the variety of loads commercially available in that gun's chambering.

Ammunition intended for defensive firearms can be evaluated in terms of five major criteria: *reliability, controllability, stopping power, accuracy* and *muzzle flash.*

RELIABILITY

Reliability refers to the ability of a firearm to consistently chamber, fire, extract and eject a particular load without malfunctions. Reliability is the single most important factor in selecting defensive ammunition. Most loads are more reliable in some guns than in others, so the only way to determine ammunition reliability is to test-fire a number of rounds through the gun being used for self-defense. Ensure that the gun is clean and well-lubricated before performing reliability testing. There's no hard and fast rule for the number of rounds that should be fired without malfunctions for the gun/ammunition combination to be considered reliable. A single box of ammunition—50 rounds—is probably not quite enough; 500 rounds might be excessive to many. Many gunsmiths recommend a defensive handgun

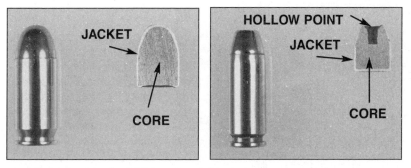

Fig. 115. A full-metal jacket (FMJ) cartridge (left) and a hollow-point cartridge. Many semi-automatic pistols are more reliable with FMJ ammunition than with hollow-point ammunition.

189

be capable of firing at least 150-200 rounds with no stoppages. The greater the number of trouble-free shots fired during reliability testing, the smaller the chance the gun will become inoperable during a confrontation. The individual gun owner must be responsible for determining the reliability standard he or she is comfortable with. A firearm that doesn't achieve that standard with at least one of the appropriate ammunition choices may need gunsmith attention.

Often, however, reliability problems in semi-automatic pistols stem from the magazine, and have little or nothing to do with the ammunition being used. By using numbered magazines, you can identify problem magazines that can be set aside, or used only for practice. Magazine-related problems may also be cured simply by trying another brand of magazine, which may be made to different tolerances or a slightly different design than the troublesome unit.

The majority of semi-automatic pistols function best with full-metal-jacket (ball) ammunition; the round-nose jacketed bullets used in such loads, however, are not the best choice for a defensive encounter. As discussed below, hollow-point bullets are the best choice for use in personal protection handguns. Hollow-points having a profile similar to that of a full-metal-jacket bullet will feed best in a self-loading pistol.

CONTROLLABILITY

Controllability is directly linked to the amount of recoil produced by a cartridge. As a general rule, the less recoil a load generates, the more controllable it will be. Controllability is important because, in defensive shooting situations, you may need more than one round to stop a violent

confrontation. This is particularly true in the case of multiple-assailant situations. The more rapidly you can make hits on an assailant, the more quickly he or she may cease the attack.

Controllability may be evaluated simply by firing several different loads and noting which one felt the softest. You may also use a shooting partner to observe the level of muzzle jump each ammunition type and brand produces; a video

Fig. 116. Ammunition that is more controllable allows a shooter to fire quick, accurate shots. Note spent case above shooter's head and in ejection port.

camera will suffice in the absence of such an observer. Additionally, timed multiple-shot drills may reveal which load allows the fastest recovery time.

STOPPING POWER

One of the most talked-about and hotly debated aspects of defensive loads, *stopping power* can be defined as the ability of a cartridge to quickly incapacitate an assailant, or otherwise cause that assailant to stop his attack. Comparisons of stopping power among different cartridges and bullet types are often made on the basis of the effects of a single well-placed shot—the often-cited "one shot stop." Despite the claims made for different bullet designs, there is a lack of complete consensus among gun authorities regarding the exact cartridge characteristics giving the best stopping power performance.

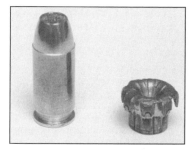

Nonetheless, some broad generalizations can be made. Hollow-point bullets usually are preferred over other types because they are designed to open up and expand in diameter upon impact. This expansion both transfers energy more efficiently to the target and also prevents overpenetration (complete penetration of the target) that could endanger the lives of others. Also, all

Fig. 117. The expansion of hollow-point bullets makes them more effective for defensive use than other bullet types.

other factors being equal, there is a rough correlation between the amount of energy the bullet has upon impact and its effectiveness in stopping an assailant.

Fortunately, you need not become a firearm expert to pick the proper ammunition. Results derived from reports of police and civilian shootings in which a single shot stopped an attacker show that virtually all of today's premium hollow-point defensive loads are adequately effective. The proper selection strategy is to pick the most reliable, controllable and accurate brand from among the variety of premium hollow-point loadings available.

ACCURACY

Although of primary importance in a gun used for target shooting or hunting, *accuracy* is only a moderately significant factor in the effectiveness of defensive handgun ammunition. This is so primarily because most defensive firearm uses take place at very close range (7 yards and under). Some authorities suggest that the ability to produce a

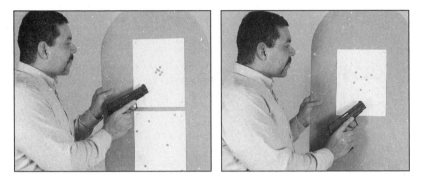

Fig. 118. Since most defensive encounters take place at relatively close range, extreme accuracy is not required. Adequate defensive accuracy is achieved when rapidly-fired shots at seven yards are reasonably centered on an 8½" by 11" piece of paper (right). The groups at left show the groups resulting from firing too slowly (top) and too quickly.

2-inch group at 7 yards is adequate for defensive purposes; the vast majority of gun and ammunition combinations will easily meet or exceed that standard. Note also that the dynamics typical of a defensive shooting situation—low light, moving targets, and a rapid firing rate—generally make any attempt at pinpoint accuracy impractical.

With fixed-sight guns, good accuracy implies more than just tight grouping; it also involves the ability of the gun and ammunition combination to shoot to the point of aim indicated by the sights. Fixed-sight arms often may be roughly adjusted for windage by drifting the rear sight laterally; elevation adjustments usually require gunsmith intervention. It is more important that defensive ammunition for such guns shoot to the point of aim; tight grouping is secondary.

MUZZLE FLASH

The *muzzle flash* generated by a load upon firing can influence the outcome of a self-defense situation, particularly at night. Under conditions of darkness, excessive flash will temporarily rob you of your night vision—the accommodation the eye has made to the low light level. The muzzle flash may also illuminate your defensive position, giving an armed attacker something to aim at.

Fig. 119. In darkness, the muzzle flash from a .357 Rem. Mag. cartridge fired from a 2"-barrel revolver would cause a loss of night vision.

The Basics of Personal Protection in the Home

SECONDARY FACTORS

In addition to the five major criteria described above, additional secondary factors should be considered in evaluating any defensive load, including its tendency to leave combustion residues, or fouling, in the barrel; whether its case can be reloaded to make a fresh cartridge (a factor of importance to reloaders); price; and availability. It is also worth noting that certain types of ammunition—particularly unusual or unconventional ammunition, or ammunition having an inflammatory or provocative brand name—have been mis-characterized by some prosecutors in an attempt to show that the person shooting in self-defense was actually eager to engage in combat and thus, inferentially, likely to shoot another person without sufficient cause.

An NRA Certified Instructor can assist you in selecting the proper defensive load for your needs.

CHAPTER 22

SELECTING FIREARM ACCESSORIES

In addition to a handgun and ammunition, there are a number of additional items that the defensive-minded gun owner should acquire.

EYE AND EAR PROTECTION

The first and foremost shooting accessories that every shooter must own are eye protection and ear protection. Both should be worn whenever engaging in live- and dry-fire practice. You should also use eye protection whenever disassembling or cleaning your firearm.

Eye protection can be afforded by specialized glasses made for shooting, certain types and styles of industrial safety glasses, and even some prescription glasses. An optician can advise you on specific designs and lens materials.

Ear protection comes in the form of ear muffs and ear plugs. Muffs are generally considered to offer somewhat better protection than plugs; however, many experienced shooters wear both for maximum sound attenuation. One of the newer and more popular ear muff designs features electronic circuitry that allows low-intensity sounds to pass unimpeded to the shooter's ear, but senses and blocks high-intensity noise, such as a gunshot.

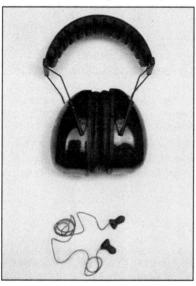

Fig. 120. Ear and eye protection are mandatory accessories for anyone who owns or shoots a firearm. Ear protection (left) helps counter the effects of gunshot noise, and most commonly can be had in the form of ear muffs or ear plugs. Maximum protection is achieved when both are worn simultaneously. Eye protection (above) should be worn whenever engaging in live-fire or dry-fire practice, or whenever disassembling or cleaning your gun. Many shooting glasses come with shatter-resistant polymer lenses in a variety of different colors.

CLEANING KIT

For proper gun maintenance, a complete cleaning kit is essential. Such a kit should contain at least the following items:
- cloth patches;
- cleaning rod with cleaning rod attachments, including bore brush and an assortment of cleaning rod tips to hold patches;
- a small brush for cleaning tight spots and crevices;
- gun cleaning solvent (bore cleaner);
- gun oil;
- a soft cloth for wiping exterior gun surfaces; and
- eye protection.

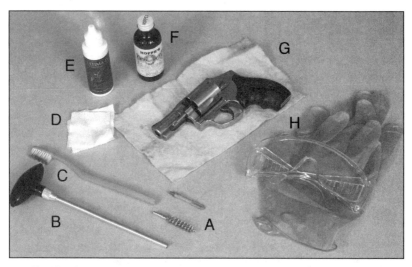

Fig. 121. The elements of a basic gun cleaning kit, including (clockwise from bottom center): (A) bronze bore brush and slotted tip for holding patches; (B) cleaning rod; (C) small brush; (D) cotton patches; (E) gun oil; (F) gun cleaning solvent; (G) soft cloth; and (H) eye protection. Also shown are thin rubber gloves, which may help protect the skin from prolonged exposure to dirt, oil and solvent.

These items may be purchased separately, or together in a kit. See Appendix A: Firearm Maintenance for more information on the tools and techniques to keep your firearm clean.

GUN STORAGE DEVICES

It is every gun owner's responsibility to ensure that his or her firearms are stored so that they are inaccessible to all persons unauthorized to

The Basics of Personal Protection in the Home

Fig. 122. Gun storage devices, including (top l.) a steel gun box with a Simplex®-type lock, (l.) a plastic case secured with a padlock, and a gun safe.

handle them. Each gun owner must make the individual choice of how that is best accomplished. In some jurisdictions, firearm storage methods are not determined by individual decision, but by local ordinance or state law. Consult a knowledgeable attorney for the legal requirements in your area.

Those gun owners who choose, or are compelled by law, to lock their firearms in gun safes or gun boxes can choose from a wide variety of sizes and types, from lightweight portable plastic cases to steel-sided gun safes that may be permanently attached to walls, cabinets and the like. Some cases have combination or keyed locks, while others, such as Simplex® locks, have numbered buttons that may be pressed in a specific sequence to allow access. This latter type of lock is often preferred for gun safes or lockboxes that are used to store personal protection firearms, because it is easier to open in the dark or under stress.

In addition to providing firearm security in a home or business, a lockable case may be required when a firearm is transported inside a vehicle, such as to a shooting range or gunsmith shop. Again, consult your attorney for the laws in your city, county or state.

SPEEDLOADERS

Speedloaders—devices that hold a cylinder-full of cartridges in position to be quickly inserted in the cylinder's chamber—afford the fastest means of recharging the chambers of a revolver cylinder. Revolver shooters should have several speedloaders to facilitate speedy reloading.

Several extra speedloaders will also permit you to practice reloading drills with one or two of the devices while retaining the remainder for an actual defensive situation. It is important to keep the practice speedloaders separate from those used for defensive purposes, because the practice units may become worn and thus less reliable from frequent use.

Fig. 123. Speedloaders reduce the time required to reload a revolver. Knob (arrow) is turned to release the cartridges when they are aligned with the chambers.

SPARE MAGAZINES

If your defensive handgun is a semi-automatic, it is important to have several extra magazines for it. Additional magazines will allow you to speedily recharge your pistol with a fresh supply of ammunition, in the event the initial magazine is exhausted.

Furthermore, it is recognized that the magazine is the weak link in any semi-automatic handgun design, as it is easy for thin-walled magazine bodies to become dented, misshapen, or otherwise nonfunctional in normal use. A supply of extra magazines allows you to have several that are employed only in practice sessions, while others can be kept in reserve only for actual defensive use. As with speedloaders, it is important to keep the practice magazines separate from those reserved for defensive purposes, as the practice units may become worn or damaged, and thus less reliable, from frequent practice use.

DUMMY ROUNDS/SNAP CAPS

Dummy rounds or snap caps (a type of dummy ammunition that uses a spring-loaded or soft plastic pad to cushion firing pin fall) are useful for dry-fire and gun-handling exercises. With certain gun designs, dry-firing can cause damage to action components; snap caps will prevent this. Consult the firearm owner's manual for more information on the recommended dry-fire procedure.

Snap caps can be used for certain live-fire exercises as well, such as the ball-and-dummy drill, in which dummy cartridges are mixed in with live rounds in a sequence not known to the shooter. The movement of the gun

The Basics of Personal Protection in the Home

when the trigger is pulled on the dummy round often reveals a tendency to flinch or otherwise anticipate the shot.

Dummy rounds and snap caps typically come in colors that clearly distinguish them from live ammunition. Plastic dummies are often in bright red or orange, and metal dummy rounds frequently feature a completely black cartridge case or a solid copper body.

Dummy rounds and snap caps can help improve the shooting fundamentals and are also useful in many gun-handling drills, such as speed reloading drills.

Fig. 124. Above, snap caps and dummy rounds in different calibers. The inset at right shows the three major types of these devices: left, a plastic snap cap with a brass head containing a spring-loaded plunger to cushion firing pin impact; center, a solid plastic dummy round; and right, a metal dummy round approximating the weight and feel of a live cartridge.

APPENDICES

FIREARM MAINTENANCE

Virtually all gun owners recognize the value of frequent firearm cleaning, inspection, and lubrication. A gun that is properly maintained at regular intervals will function more reliably, shoot more accurately and last longer than one whose care is neglected. While a well-maintained firearm is desirable for the complete enjoyment of such activities as plinking, hunting and and competitive shooting, it is absolutely essential in a self-defense situation, in which a single stoppage can have fatal consequences.

The critical role of a self-defense firearm demands a more rigorous schedule of maintenance than might be observed with a handgun used only to plink at tin cans on weekends. This schedule includes regular cleaning, inspection and lubrication, as well as a periodic gunsmith check-up.

CLEANING YOUR FIREARM

A gun that is shot on a regular basis accumulates dirt, powder residue and other foreign matter, all of which can make a gun more prone to stoppage, wear and corrosion. Even a firearm that is left untouched on a

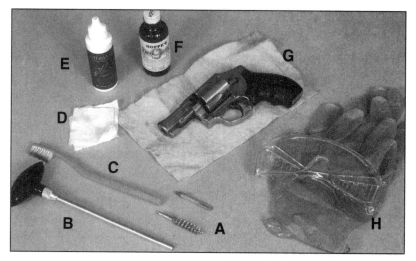

Fig. 125. The components of a basic gun cleaning kit, including (A) a bore brush and slotted tip for holding cleaning patches, (B) a cleaning rod, (C) a small brush, (D) cotton cleaning patches, (E) gun oil, (F) gun cleaning solvent, (G) a soft cloth, and (H) eye protection. Also shown are thin rubber gloves, which may help protect the skin from dirt, oil and solvent.

shelf or in a drawer can accumulate sufficient dust and dirt to affect proper functioning. Removing such harmful material is critical to ensure gun reliability and readiness.

Every gun owner should have a gun cleaning kit consisting of the following items:

- cloth patches;
- a cleaning rod and cleaning rod attachments, including a bore brush and tips to hold patches;
- a small brush (for cleaning gun crevices) ;
- gun solvent (bore cleaner);
- gun oil; and
- a soft cloth.

Kits containing all or most of these items are commercially available at any gun shop and many hardware, sporting goods and large discount stores. Make sure that any kit or individual cleaning rod, jag (a tip designed specifically to hold a cleaning patch) or bore brush is intended for a handgun in the caliber of your pistol or revolver. Also, select patches of the proper size for your bore.

In addition to the above items, you also need safety glasses to protect your eyes from cleaning solvents and spring-loaded parts that you may inadvertently dislodge from your gun. Also recommended are thin rubber gloves to protect your skin from exposure to solvents, lubricants, firing residues and lead particles. Be sure that your gun-cleaning area has good ventilation, and do not eat, drink or smoke while performing firearm maintenance.

The first step in cleaning your firearm is to ensure that it is *unloaded* (A). There should be no live ammunition in the cleaning area.

Next, disassemble your firearm according to the instructions in the owner's manual for the gun. If you do not have an owner's manual for your firearm, you can usually obtain one from the firearm's manufacturer. Alternatively, a professional gunsmith may be able to show you how to

The Basics of Personal Protection in the Home

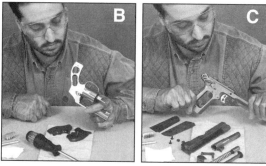

disassemble your gun. With a revolver, recommended disassembly may involve nothing more than swinging out the cylinder and removing the stocks (B). Disassembling a semi-automatic pistol usually involves the separation of the slide from the frame, which also may allow the removal of the barrel and recoil spring assembly (C). On many semi-autos, caution must be exercised to prevent a compressed recoil spring from flying free when the slide and frame are disassembled. Generally, no further disassembly is needed for normal cleaning (nor is usually recommended in the owner's manual).

Actual cleaning starts with the bore. Attach a tip to the cleaning rod (D), put a clean patch onto the jag and wet the patch with gun cleaning solvent. Push the patch slowly through the bore to saturate the bore surface and loosen powder residue, lead or copper fouling, or other unwanted material. If you are cleaning a revolver, or a semi-automatic pistol whose barrel was not removed, you will probably have to push the patch through from the muzzle end (E). When cleaning from the muzzle end of the barrel, avoid rubbing the cleaning rod against the bore to prevent accuracy-robbing wear on the rifling. If you are cleaning a semi-automatic pistol whose barrel was removed as part of disassembly, push the patch through from the chamber (rearmost) end (F).

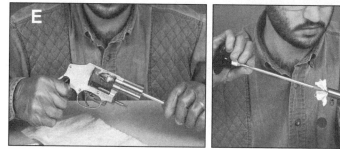

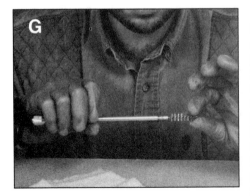

Next, attach the bore brush to the cleaning rod and moisten it with gun cleaning solvent (G). If possible, use a dropper to put solvent onto the brush; avoid dipping the brush in the solvent, as this contaminates the clean solvent with dirt and grit on the brush. Push the brush all the way through the bore, then pull it back through the bore (H). Do not try to reverse direction with the brush still in the bore. Run the brush through the bore about 15-20 times, adding solvent as necessary.

Re-attach the jag to the cleaning rod and push a clean, dry patch through the bore (I). This patch will come out quite dirty with the material

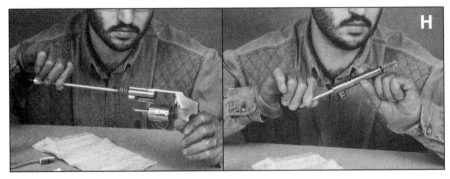

that was loosened by the solvent and the bore brush. Run more dry patches through the bore; they should come out progressively cleaner, until virtually no fouling is visible (J). If the patches keep coming out somewhat dirty, repeat the cleaning process as outlined in the previous paragraphs.

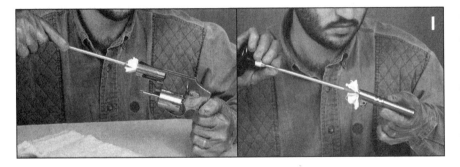

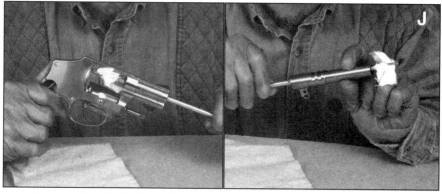

Also, visually check the surface of the bore for any remaining fouling, lead, or powder residue.

In cleaning a revolver, the cylinders are cleaned using much the same technique as is employed in cleaning the bore (K).

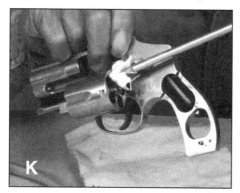

Once the bore is clean, residue must be removed from other gun surfaces. Use a solvent-soaked patch, cotton swab or toothbrush, as appropriate, to loosen and remove powder residue and other matter from working surfaces. On a semi-automatic pistol, such surfaces include the interior of the slide, the slide and frame rails, and the exterior barrel surface. On a revolver, such surfaces include the crane, frame, and any action parts that are made accessible by the removal of the stocks (L).

Maintenance of semi-automatic pistol magazines is critical for proper pistol functioning. Most magazines are designed to be disassembled; instructions should be in your owner's manual. Once the magazine is disassembled, push patches through the magazine body to clean out loose dirt, powder residue and other matter (M).

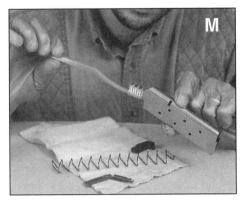

In most cases, the owner's manual will present only those disassembly instructions required to perform basic cleaning and maintenance; more complete disassembly of the firearm is usually discouraged. However, dirt and powder residue can also collect in interior action areas that can be accessed only by complete disassembly. A partial cleaning of these inaccessible areas may be achieved by flushing the action with gun cleaner or a solvent that leaves no residue, such as brake cleaner. The solvent is sprayed into the action in such a way as to allow the excess to drain freely (such as with the stocks removed), dissolving and flushing away loosened dirt and residue.

INSPECTING YOUR FIREARM

The ideal time for giving your firearm a thorough visual inspection is when it is disassembled after cleaning. Defects are easiest to spot on parts that are free of dirt, residue and oil. Look for cracks, burred, pitted or indented areas, broken parts and so forth. Also be aware of screws or pins that have worked loose, sights that have drifted from recoil forces, or parts that seem to have shifted from their normal positions.

Additionally, every time you pick up your firearm, whether to practice at the range, dry-fire in your basement, or clean it in your workroom, you should give it a cursory inspection (after, of course, making sure it is unloaded). Look for the buildup of firing residues; grips screws or other parts that have become loose; excessive oil leaking out of the joints between parts; and any other condition that may affect the function of the gun. Getting in the habit of making this kind of inspection will help you determine when cleaning or lubrication is necessary, or if there are any conditions that may make your gun unsafe or unreliable.

LUBRICATING YOUR FIREARM

Cleaning powder residues and other foreign material from the gun usually removes necessary lubrication from working surfaces. Thus, it is

The Basics of Personal Protection in the Home

essential to re-lubricate the firearm after it has been cleaned.

The owner's manual for your gun likely contains detailed instructions on the proper method of lubrication. In general, lubricate revolvers in the areas of the crane, ejector rod, and cylinder latch, and around the sides of the hammer and trigger. With the stocks removed, you may also squirt oil into action areas to smooth the trigger pull.

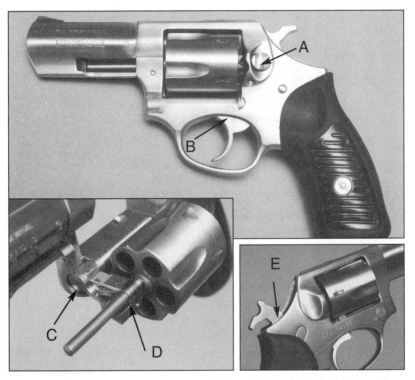

Fig. 126. Lubrication points for a revolver include the cylinder latch (A), the junction of the trigger and the frame (B), the crane (C), the ejector rod (D), and alongside the hammer where it meets the frame (E). With the hammer back, a few drops of oil may also be dripped into the action to lubricate internal action parts. Internal parts may also be accessed for lubrication by removing the stocks.

Semi-automatic pistols should be lubricated on the slide and frame rails, at the muzzle (where the barrel articulates with the slide), and in the barrel locking area. Also apply a small amount of oil to the sides of the trigger and hammer where they enter the frame, to smooth their movement.

Additionally, drip a small amount of lubricant into action areas, particularly around the trigger and hammer pins. If you desire, you may put a very light film of oil on the exterior surface of the magazines to prevent rust and to

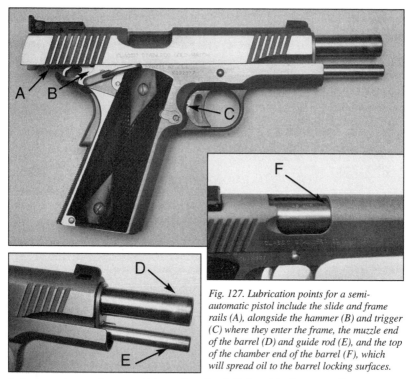

Fig. 127. Lubrication points for a semi-automatic pistol include the slide and frame rails (A), alongside the hammer (B) and trigger (C) where they enter the frame, the muzzle end of the barrel (D) and guide rod (E), and the top of the chamber end of the barrel (F), which will spread oil to the barrel locking surfaces.

help insertion and removal from the pistol. It is critical not to allow oil to be transferred to the cartridges carried within the magazine. Oil on cartridge cases can penetrate to the primer, making its ignition less reliable, and may have other negative effects on gun functioning as well.

It is important to use only those lubricants designed expressly for use in firearms. Over time, improper lubricants may become gummy, impairing proper gun functioning, or may be too thin or runny to provide lasting protection. Also, firearms that are used in climates that are extremely hot, cold, wet or dusty often have very special lubrication needs, as do firearms that will be stored for extended periods. Consult with a gun shop or gunsmith to determine the proper lubricants to be used with your firearm.

It is also important to avoid over-lubricating your handgun, or leaving oil in certain areas. For example, while a thin film of oil should coat the bore of a firearm that is to be stored, all oil must be removed from the bore before the gun is fired. Also, excess lubricant can penetrate wood stocks and cause them to deteriorate, and too much oil left inside the magazine of a semi-automatic pistol or the chambers of a revolver cylinder can contaminate cartridge primers and lead to misfires.

FUNCTION CHECKING YOUR FIREARM

After cleaning, inspecting and lubricating the firearm, the final stage is reassembly and function checking. The inspection process alluded to previously should continue during reassembly. Be aware of parts that do not go together as they should, a sudden increase in the play or looseness of pins and other components, and so forth.

When the firearm is reassembled, *make sure that it is unloaded* and then dry-fire it a few times to see if there are any changes in the feel of the trigger or the functioning of the controls. With a revolver, swing the cylinder out and test the action of the extractor rod. Rack the slide of a semiautomatic and ensure that its various safety controls are functioning. Don't just look with your eyes; listen with your ears. Sometimes the sound of the gun as it is cycled or dry-fired can reveal a functional problem.

Similarly, when firing live ammunition at the range, be aware of any changes in the gun's function or feel. A sudden tendency of the gun to misfire, jam, or change the tightness or location of its groups may be a sign of a mechanical problem.

Changes in gun function are sometimes the result of a buildup of dirt, powder residue, congealed lubricant and so forth. This is

Fig. 128. Always function check a firearm without ammunition after it has been disassembled for cleaning or repair. Here a shooter works the slide of a semi-automatic pistol.

especially true of jams or sluggishness in cycling that occur gradually when many rounds have been fired without maintenance. In such cases, proper functioning is often restored by a thorough cleaning and lubrication.

On the other hand, problems in functioning that appear suddenly or are not rectified by cleaning may indicate a broken part or other serious condition. In such cases, consult a gunsmith.

OTHER MAINTENANCE

Firearm maintenance involves more than just cleaning, inspection, lubrication and function testing. Both semi-automatic pistols and revolvers are powered by springs, which can, over time, fatigue and impair functioning. The springs that power revolver hammers generally last for many years before they weaken enough to cause problems; however,

revolvers having a tendency to produce light hits on the primer may be suffering from weak springs. A gunsmith can help diagnose and remedy this problem.

Recoil springs on semi-automatic pistols should be replaced at regular intervals, usually every several thousand rounds. Your owner's manual should have specific recommendations regarding recoil spring replacement, as well as directions for installing new springs. A gunsmith can also assist you in replacing recoil springs.

The weak link of the semi-automatic pistol is its magazine. While most magazine springs are designed to retain their stiffness for long periods, even when left compressed, some magazine

Fig. 129. Performing regular maintenance, such as the replacement of fatigued recoil springs (above), is a part of responsible firearm ownership.

springs will fatigue over time. Some feeding problems may result from improper magazine spring tension; a gunsmith can diagnose this condition.

GUNSMITH CHECK-UP

In addition to the normal maintenance you can perform, it is important to periodically have a gunsmith completely disassemble, clean inspect and lubricate your firearm. This is also an opportunity for an experienced eye to look for wear, breakage or other conditions that may affect your gun's ability to defend you or your loved ones.

The frequency of this kind of gunsmith examination depends upon your shooting habits. In general, if you practice regularly with your firearm, an annual check-up is indicated.

The Basics of Personal Protection in the Home

APPENDIX B

INFORMATION AND TRAINING RESOURCES

The following is not meant to be an exhaustive list of the books, magazines, videos and training opportunities available to today's gun owners. Instead, it is only a representative sampling of these resources. Inclusion of a resource in the list below does not imply NRA endorsement of its contents. Consult an NRA Certified Instructor for further information on additional resources that may be available to you.

BOOKS

Armed and Considered Dangerous: A Survey of Felons and Their Firearms, by James D. Wright and Peter H. Rossi. Aldine de Gruyter, Hawthorne, NY, 1994. ISBN 0-202-30542-2

Armed and Female, by Paxton Quigley. E.P. Dutton & Co., New York, NY, 1989. ISBN 0-225-24742-4

The Basics of Pistol Shooting. National Rifle Association of America, Fairfax, VA, 1991.

Best Defense: True Stories of Intended Victims Who Defended Themselves with a Firearm, by Robert Waters. Cumberland House Publishing, Nashville, TN, 1998. ISBN 1-888952-97-0

Concealed Handgun Manual, by Chris Bird. Privateer Publishing, San Antonio, TX, 2000. ISBN 0-9656784-6-6

Defensive Shotgun, by Louis Awerbuck. Desert Publishing, El Dorado, AR, 1989. ISBN 0-87947-412-2

Effective Defense—The Woman, The Plan, The Gun, by Gila May Hayes. FAS Books, Onalaska, WA, 1994. ISBN 1-885036-01-9

The Freedmen, The Fourteenth Amendment and the Right to Bear Arms, 1866-1876, by Stephen P. Halbrook. Greenwood Publishing Group, Westport, CT, 1998. ISBN 0-275-96331-4

Gun Control and the Constitution: Sources and Explorations on the Second Amendment, ed. by Robert Cottrol. Garland Publishing, Inc., Hamden, CT. ISBN 0-8153-1666-6

Guns, Bullets and Gunfights, by Jim Cirillo. Paladin Press, Boulder, CO, 1996. ISBN 0-87364-877-3

The Gun Digest Book of Combat Hangunnery, 5th Edition, by Massad Ayoob, Krause Publications, Iola, WI, 2002,. ISBN 0-87349-485-7

In the Gravest Extreme, The Role of the Firearm in Personal Protection, by Massad Ayoob, Police Bookshelf, Concord, NH, 1980. ISBN 0-936297-00-1

Guns, Crime and Freedom, by Wayne Lapierre. Regnery Publishing, Washington, DC, 1994. ISBN 0-89526-477-3

Home Firearm Safety. National Rifle Association of America, Fairfax, VA, 1996.

Kill or Get Killed, by Rex Applegate. Paladin Press, Boulder, CO, 1976. ISBN 0-87364-084-5

More Guns, Less Crime, by John Lott. University of Chicago Press, Chicago, 1998. ISBN 0-226-49363-6

NRA Firearm Fact Book. National Rifle Association, Fairfax, VA, 1994. ISBN 0-935998-55-1

Winchester/NRA Marksmanship Qualification Program (booklet). National Rifle Association, Fairfax, VA, 2000.

Origins and Development of the Second Amendment, by David Hardy. Blacksmith Corp., North Hampton, OH, 1986. ISBN 0-941540-13-8

Principles of Personal Defense, by Jeff Cooper. Paladin Press, Boulder CO, 1988. ISBN 0-87364-497-2

Smart & Safe: Handling Your Firearm (booklet). National Rifle Association of America, Fairfax, VA, 2000.

Stressfire, by Massad Ayoob. Police Bookshelf, Concord, NH, 1986. ISBN 0-936279-03-6

Tactical Advantage, by Gabriel Suarez. Paladin Press, Boulder, CO, 1998. ISBN 0-87364-975-3

Tactical Pistol, by Gabriel Suarez. Paladin Press, Boulder, CO, 1996. ISBN 0-87364-864-1

Tactical Reality, by Louis Awerbuck. Paladin Press, Boulder, CO, 1999. ISBN 0-58160-051-8

That Every Man Be Armed: The Evolution of a Constitutional Right, by Stephen P. Halbrook. Independent Institute, Oakland, CA, 1994. ISBN 0-945999-38-0

The Truth About Handguns, by Duane Thomas. Paladin Press, Boulder, CO, 1997. ISBN 0-87364-953-2

Up To Speed, by John Mattera. Zediker Publishing, Oxford, MS, 1998. ISBN 0-9626925-8-1

MAGAZINES

All titles below published monthly by the National Rifle Association of America, Fairfax, VA.

American Rifleman
America's 1st Freedom
American Hunter
Shooting Illustrated
Shooting Sports USA
InSights

VIDEOS

Fundamentals of Gun Safety: The Basic Rules of Safe Firearm Ownership.
National Rifle Association of America, Fairfax, VA, 1991.

A Woman's Guide to Firearms.
Lyon House Productions, Hollywood, CA, 1987.

TRAINING

Consult an NRA Certified Instructor for information on further training opportunities to enhance your knowledge, skills and attitude. (703) 267-1430.

COMPETITION

The following competitive activities (listed with their sanctioning organizations) are among those that will develop shooting and gun handling skills that are relevant to defensive shooting.

NRA Action Pistol: Competitive Shooting Division, National Rifle Association of America, 11250 Waples Mill Road, Fairfax, VA 22030, (703) 267-1450.

IDPA (International Defensive Pistol Association): 2232 CR 719, Berryville, AK 72616, (870) 545-3886.

IPSC (International Practical Shooting Confederation: 903A Metcalf St., Sedro Wooley, WA 98284, (360) 855-2245.

APPENDIX C

FACTS ABOUT THE NRA

Established in 1871, the National Rifle Association of America (NRA) is a non-profit organization supported entirely by membership fees and by donations from public-spirited citizens.

Originally formed to promote marksmanship training, the NRA has since reached out to establish a wide variety of activities, ranging from gun safety programs for children and adults to gun collecting and gunsmithing. Hundreds of thousands of law enforcement and civilian personnel have received training from NRA Certified Instructors in the firearm skills needed to protect themselves and the public. In addition, clubs enrolled or affiliated with the NRA exist in communities across the nation, teaching youths and adults gun safety, marksmanship, and responsibility while also providing recreational activities.

The membership of the NRA has included eight Presidents of the United States, two Chief Justices of the U.S. Supreme Court, and many of America's most outstanding diplomats, military leaders, members of Congress, and other public officials.

The NRA helps train shooters to compete in numerous forms of shooting competition at the local, state, regional, national and international levels.

The NRA provides numerous training and educational programs.

The NRA also cooperates with federal agencies, all branches of the U.S. Armed Forces, and state and local governments that are interested in training and safety programs.

The basic goals of the NRA are to:

• Protect and defend the Constitution of the United States, especially in regard to the Second Amendment right of the individual citizen to keep and bear arms
• Promote public safety, law and order, and the national defense
• Train citizens and members of law enforcement agencies and the armed forces in the safe handling and efficient use of firearms
• Foster and promote the shooting sports at local, state regional, national, and international levels
• Promote hunter safety and proper wildlife management

The NRA does not receive any appropriations from Congress, nor is it a trade organization. It is not affiliated with any gun or ammunition manufacturers, or with any businesses which deal in guns or ammunition.

To join NRA today, or for additional information regarding membership, please call 1-800-NRA-3888. Your membership dues can be charged to VISA, Master Card, American Express or Discover.

To contact the NRA for assistance or additional information, please direct all inquiries to:
National Rifle Association of America
11250 Waples Mill Road
Fairfax, VA 22030
(703) 267-1000 (Main Switchboard)

For questions relating to specific NRA divisions, send mail inquiries directly to the attention of those divisions at the above address, or use the following telephone numbers:

Competitive Shooting Division
Tournament Operations
Rifle Department
Collegiate and Schools Department
NRA Disabled Shooting Services
Silhouette and Black Powder
Pistol and Support Programs
(703) 267-1450

Education & Training Division
Training Department (Instructor/Coach,
    Youth, Women on Target
    Programs)
Sports Department (Hunting, Clubs &
    Assoc., Ranges, Recreational
    Shooting)
Community Outreach (Eddie Eagle®,
    Refuse To Be A Victim®)
(703) 267-1500

Field Operations Division
Field Representatives
Volunteer Fund-Raising
(703) 267-1340

General Counsel's Office
(703) 267-1250

Institute for Legislative Action
ILA—Conservation Wildlife & Natural Resources
(703) 267-1541
ILA—Grassroots
(703) 267-1170

ILA—Communications
(703) 267-3820
ILA—State & Local
(703) 267-1236

Law Enforcement Activities Division
Technical Information
Police Competitions
Police Training
Special Firearms
(703) 267-1640

Membership Division
All locations except Wash. Metro Area
(703) 267-3700
(800) NRA-3888

Museum/Gun Collecting Program
Gun Collecting Program
Museum
(703) 267-1600

Publications Division
American Hunter
American Rifleman
America's 1st Freedom
InSights
Shooting Sports USA
(703) 267-1300

Members' Insurance
Life, Accident, & Health
(800) 247-7989

Property & Liability Insurance
Lockton Risk Services
Arms Care Plus
Excess Personal Liability
Firearms Instructors
Self-Defense
Club Property & Liability
Business Owner's Insurance
(877) 487-5407

NRA Program Materials Center
(800) 336-7402
Order on-line at: http://materials.nrahq.org

Technical Questions

Receiving answers to technical questions is a privilege reserved for NRA members. (A non-member may submit a question if the inquiry is accompanied by a membership application.) Each question must be in the form of a letter addressed to:

Dope Bag
NRA Publications
11250 Waples Mill Road
Fairfax, VA 22030

Each inquiry must contain the NRA member's code line from his or her membership card or from the mailing label on the *American Rifleman*, *American Hunter*, or *America's 1st Freedom* magazine. Inquiries must be limited to one specific question per letter. Questions regarding the value of any type of firearm will not be accepted. In addition, each inquiry must include a stamped, self-addressed, legal-size envelope. No technical questions will be answered by telephone, e-mail or fax.

INDEX